TaRYaG

TaRYaG

A STUDY
OF THE
TRADITION
THAT THE
WRITTEN
TORAH
CONTAINS
613 MITZVOT

Abraham
Hirsch Rabinowitz

JASON ARONSON INC.
Northvale, New Jersey
London

This book was set in 12 pt. Cheltenham Book by AeroType, Inc., of Amherst, New Hampshire.

Library of Congress Cataloging-in-Publication Data

Rabinowitz, Abraham Hirsch.
   TaRYaG : a study of the tradition that the written Torah contains
  613 mitzvot / Abraham Hirsch Rabinowitz.
      p. cm.
  Previously published: Jerusalem : Hillel Press, 1967.
  Includes bibliographical references and index.
  ISBN 1-56821-449-9 (alk. paper)
   1. Commandments, Six hundred and thirteen—History of doctrines.
 I. Title.
 BM520.8.R224 1996
 296.1'8—dc20   96-22408
                                                      CIP

Manufactured in the United States of America. Jason Aronson Inc. offers books and cassettes. For information and catalog write to Jason Aronson Inc., 230 Livingston Street, Northvale, New Jersey 07647.

To My Dear Parents In-Law
The Gaon Rabbi Issachar Tamar
and Rabbanit Sarah Freidel Tamar
of Tel Aviv

Contents

Contents

Introduction

The fact that the Written Torah contains 613 precepts is generally known and accepted. This study attempts to investigate the major problems connected with the tradition. The origin of the tradition is carefully investigated as is the word "precept" in this connection, while the influence of the tradition and the use to which it was put during almost two millenia of Jewish history is outlined.

Various modern scholars have discussed the tradition. Resulting, however, from their failure to discover its fundamental basis and meaning, their treatment of it was cursory and in some instances fanciful. The attempts on the part of these scholars to find the origin of the tradition in a historical tract, originally formulated as an educational device, or in numerical symbolism is shown to be unfounded. The concept of TaRYaG is grounded in Halachah, which alone is responsible for the importance and historical development of the tradition.

The greatest scholars of Israel contributed studies on this tradition. The present study shows clearly why the tradition merited their attention to such a considerable extent. It also analyzes not only the particular motive and style of each author, but also his individual approach to the subject. Maimonides' epoch treatise the *Sefer HaMitzvot* is fully analyzed and its relationship to his magnum opus *Mishneh Torah* is clearly shown for the first time.

The linking of TaRYaG with the Decalogue and the inherent popularity of the tradition resulted in its having entered the liturgy. It was found to be an excellent medium for popular instruction in the Oral Law and was put to fruitful use in this context since the organic relationship between the written and oral laws emerges clearly from study of the TaRYaG tradition; while in the hands of the great masters and codifiers of Halachah it provided the forum for the scientific analysis of the entire halachic literature of the Rabbis.

1

The Historical Problem

The Talmud[1] states:

> R. Simlai[2] explained,[3] 613[4] precepts were revealed unto Moses at Sinai, 365 prohibitive precepts, like the number of days in the solar year,[5] and 248 positive precepts corresponding to the number of limbs[6] in the human body.[7]

---

1. *Makkot* 23b.
2. Ja'abetz, in his *History*, pt. 7, p. 36 n. 1, considers the name to be Samlai. Cf. also Bacher Aggadoth Amoraim, pt. 2, p. 318 n. 1.
3. Heb. *Darash*, in opposition to Bacher, ibid., who maintains that R. Simlai was mainly a teacher of Haggaddah, Ja'abetz, ibid., shows that he was also an eminent halachist.
4. The number is usually known by the Hebrew mnemonic TaR-YaG, T = 400, R = 200, Y = 10, G = 3, and this mnemonic is used throughout the present work.
5. Cf. Tanchuma, ed. Buber, sec. *Thetze*, para. 2.
6. See Soncino Talmud, ad loc. n. 5. Ch. Heller in his critical edition of

The tradition, contained in this passage, that the Torah contains 613 mitzvot gives rise to a major problem. For a simple enumeration proves that the actual number of the positive and prohibitive precepts far exceeds TaRYaG.[8] Yet the number TaRYaG has always been considered axiomatic. The earliest sources take it for granted, and throughout the centuries of literary controversy to which the tradition gave rise, hardly any scholar seriously impugned the validity of the tradition.[9] How, then, is one to understand the tradition?

Maimonides' *Sefer HaMitzvot* (NY, 1946), preface p. 4 n. 49, remarks that the oft-quoted statement that "the 365 prohibitions parallel the 365 sinews in the human body" is found nowhere in the Talmud and has its origin in the *Zohar*. See also D. Margalit, *Sinai* 20: 2 (October 1956). Minyan HaMitzvoth Vehaevarim Vehagiddim Shebagguff.

7. For the variant readings of this important passage see Bacher, p. 322 n. 1, Heller n. 51, and Root One p. 5 n. 1, at length. See also Tanchuma, Buber, end Shofetim, where the phrase "Said R. Simlai, 613 mitzvot were told to Moses at Sinai" appears, thus allowing for the surmise that this is the original statement of R. Simlai, the remainder being an addition by others. If this is indeed the original statement of R. Simlai, no further argument is necessary in order to refute the symbolic interpretation of the passage in *Makkot*, offered by Shechter and others (see below, this chapter).

8. This is evidenced by the fact that if the lists of positive precepts alone, suggested by various authorities, are collated, one finds no less than five hundred mitzvot considered for inclusion in R. Simlai's 248, while Maimonides mentions in Root Three that there are no less than three hundred precepts of a temporary nature in the Torah.

9. Nachmanides in his First Root discusses the validity of the tradition at length. In spite of a lurking doubt, he concludes that it was indeed the genuine opinion of the Rabbis that the number of precepts in the Torah is TaRYaG. I. S. Hurwitz, in his commentary to the *Sefer HaMitzvot* of Maimonides Jerusalem: Yad Halevi, 1931), goes further than any other scholar in impugning the validity of this tradition, and he is of the opinion that the tradition does not reflect the true opinion of the Rabbis of the Talmud. Sufficient evidence will be brought during the course of this study to show clearly the untenability of his position.

It is true that the Torah contains many more than 613 laws; and if one considers those laws derived by means of the hermeneutic rules applied by the Rabbis when studying Torah,[10] bearing in mind that each law deduced by their means is regarded as valid biblical law,[11] the number runs into many thousands.[12] Nevertheless distinguishing characteristics do exist and it is with these in mind that the tradition singles out 613 mitzvot.[13]

Mentioning TaRYaG mitzvot, the tradition, in addition to giving a definite number for the precepts, conveys a concept. There is no intention to exclude or minimize other biblical obligations.[14] On the contrary, all the manifold laws of the Torah are conceived of as being grouped under classified heads in the sense of branches spreading from the trunk of a tree.[15] Understood thus, the tradition reduces the vast complex of Torah law to analytical treatment. The numerous details of Torah legislation may be arranged under their appropriate headings and a complete picture of every facet of Torah life achieved.[16]

---

10. See The Fathers according to R. Nathan, chap. 37; and opening chapter of the Sifra.

11. The fact is self-evident for the student of the Talmud. See also chap. 2 at length.

12. The Talmud itself states that no less than 1,700 laws were forgotten during the period of mourning for Moses (*Temurah* 16a).

13. See chaps. 2 and 7.

14. For the purpose of this study "mitzvah" is to be understood in the limited sense of "an observance or a prohibition that fulfills the conditions necessary for inclusion among the 613 mitzvot mentioned by R. Simlai."

15. Yeraim (see here pp. 1000) states in his preface: the written mitzvot I called Avot—primary, the additions of the sages "Toldot"—derivative. Cf. similar usage B.K. Ra., etc.

16. Cf. Maimonides' preface to his *Sefer HaMitzvot* (S.H.). See next note.

Unfortunately, apart from stating that such heads exist, early tradition gives no criteria for ascertaining their identity. In the entire corpus of Tannaitic, talmudic and midrashic literature, no more than hints are to be found as to how a member of TaRYaG is to be defined. Even a cursory acquaintance with Halachah and its ramifications is sufficient to make one realize the complexity of the problem. Some criteria had to be evolved and applied to thousands of biblical laws, and it was not until Maimonides wrote his epoch treatise the "Fourteen Roots"[17] as an introduction to his *Sefer HaMitzvot*[18] that the problem began to be studied scientifically.[19]

17. This treatise, and in fact the entire S.H. is the product of chance rather than design. Maimonides, in his preface to the S.H., tells us that he only came to write on the subject at all because of his intention to compile the *Mishneh Torah* (See here chap. 6). He realized that the execution of this monolithic task required some sort of ground plan if it were to succeed, and this led him to create and use the S.H. as the base. In examining the works that had until then appeared on the subject, he detected numerous errors and wrote the "Fourteen Roots" in order to refute the attempts to enumerate TaRYaG that had preceded him. Incidentally, this treatise is the only work of Maimonides in which the student is able to study the Master's methods of study. It deserves, therefore, the most careful attention of all interested in Maimonides and his work.

18. An interesting and thorough discussion of the actual title of Maimonides' work on TaRYaG is to be found in Neubauer, HaRaMbaM Al Divrei Sopherim (Jerusalem, 1957), p. 91 et seq., who shows that the work has been variously called by different authorities. Ibn Tibbon, in his introduction, calls it a "Maamar," Maimonides himself, in a celebrated responsum to R. Pinchass Meshullam (ed. Friemann, (Jerusalem, 1934) calls it his "Hibbur BeInyan HaMitzvot." Abarbanel calls it simply "Minyan HaMitzvot," as does the seventeenth-century historian David Conforte.

19. Predecessors of Maimonides, notably Chefetz b. Yazliach, did study the subject scientifically, but his work has not survived. See here chap. 5.

But even with the epoch work of Maimonides, an absolute[20] list of TaRYaG has not been forthcoming. Maimonides himself wrote two editions of his work. In the first, seven precepts were missing, which but illustrates the difficulties that remained in spite of his logical system.[21] Scholars have debated the question for centuries but no list has been determined upon against which there are no objections.[22]

Nachmanides, at the end of his *Book of Precepts*,[23] writes:

20. Ibn Ezra, in his *Yesod Morah*, chap. 2, in inveighing chiefly against the compilers of the Azharot, (see here chap. 4), employs logical arguments against all systems of enumeration. He was preceded in his criticism by Judah Ibn Baal'am in his commentary to Deuteronomy 30 (ed. Fuchs). See B. Z. Halper, *Jewish Quarterly Review* (April 1914): 525. Incidentally, when Halper says there that "subsequent writers like Moses of Coucy follow Maimonides with but few deviations," he is mistaken. Moses of Coucy never saw the S.H. of Maimonides. See Heller, Introduction p. 2, and also Isaiah Hurwitz, *Shenei Luchoth Habrith,* vol. 3 (Warsaw, 1852), p. 117.

21. See R. Shimeon b. R. Zemach Duran, *Zohar Harakia* (Vilna, 1878), end. But see Heller Introduction to Second Edition, pp. 23–25.

22. Meiri, thirteenth-century scholar of Provence, in his commentary to *Makkot,* ed. S. Waxman (New York, 1950), p. 115, says "the details of those mitzvot included in the 613 have become muddled at the hands of the commentators." Heller (introduction) declared that Meiri, who otherwise continually quotes Maimonides' works, had not apparently seen his S.H. since he never refers to it. He must, however, certainly have been aware of its existence; see Beth Habechirah ad loc.

23. It is a commonly held mistake that Nachmanides composed his work as a commentary to that of Maimonides, under the title *Hassagot HaRamBan,* Nachmanides' Refutations. Maggid Mishneh (Ishuth chap. 1, *Challah* 2 and other instances) states that Nachmanides wrote his work as a commentary to the S.H., but Nachmanides himself never refers to his "Sepher Hassagoth," which would support this view. He refers only to his *Sefer HaMitzvot.* Many responsa, including those of RaShbA, Nachmanides' pupil, refer to the latter's *Sepher HaMitzvot,* as does Aaron of Barcelona in his famous Chinuch, Mitzvah 4, etc. See also Neubauer, p. 100, and Heller, (introduction note) 4. C. B. Chavell,

In truth the matter of listing the precepts is one concerning which I doubt all of us (i.e., those who have
engaged upon this matter). I leave the true elucidation
of the mitzvot to him of whom it is said, all doubts are
at rest . . . Elijah will explain this matter.[24]

In spite of the difficulties involved in enumerating
TaRYaG, the list of works enumerating the precepts continued to grow, aided not a little by the widespread popularity
of the azharot.[25] The challenge of TaRYaG engaged the
mind and pen of Israel's greatest, but subsequent literature
failed to equal Maimonides' accomplishment.[26]

It is pertinent to understand the reasons that prompted
the Rabbis of the Talmud in their failure to reduce a widely
accepted tradition to factual terms.[27]

The Book of Divine Precepts (Soncino, 1940), Foreword p. xxii is also
mistaken in this connection.

24. Duran expresses similar doubts at the conclusion of his Zohar
Harakia.

25. The azharah was a liturgical poem with TaRYaG as its theme
and was recited regularly in the synagogue services for Pentecost. See
chap. 4.

26. Quite apart from the actual enumeration of TaRYaG, Maimonides' work contributed enormously to the fundamental understanding of Halachah as a whole. Side by side with the TaRYaG literature has
proceeded research into halachic principle. In my opinion it may not
be too much to say that this latter is the most important achievement of
the entire TaRYaG literature, having given rise as it did to the science of
Halachah.

27. In other instances involving numbers, the Rabbis did not fail to
elucidate, e.g., Mishnah Shabbat 7:2, where the thirty-nine classes of
work are enumerated. Chullin 3:1, where the eighteen classes of Trefah
are enumerated. Oholoth 1:8, where the 248 limbs of the body are
enumerated, etc. Cf. also Jerusalem Shekalim, chap. 5, Challah 2, on
the Sopherim and their work.

It has been conjectured[28] that the origin of the number lay in an educational device and was used as such in the early Tannaitic period. That is to say that a list of TaRYaG in fact existed and was used in the primary school education of children.

The fact that no such text has survived does not necessarily refute this view, since numerous early Tannaitic texts have perished.

This theory, however, is open to doubt on the following grounds. It is well nigh inconceivable, if such a list in fact existed at that early period and forms the basis of the TaRYaG tradition, that no mention should have been made of it throughout the entire corpus of rabbinic literature, in the pages of which reference is made to so many "lost" texts.[29]

Further, although it might be thought consistent with a system of learning grounded upon committing an Oral Law to memory to learn such a list by heart, there is no evidence to suggest that the Bible itself was so committed to memory or that it was required to learn any of its contents by heart. On the contrary, the Rabbis were particularly strict in applying the rule of "that which is written is forbidden to be recited orally,"[30] as well as its converse.[31]

---

28. L. Blau, "Lehren and Gruppieren der Gebote in Talmudischer Zeit," Soncino Blatter, 3, pp. 113–128. Quoted by Salo Baron, *The Jewish Community,* 2nd ed., vol. 2, p. 421 n. 51.

29. Jerusalem *Megillah* 5:1, Jerusalem *Berakhot* 9, Jerusalem *Taanit* 6:4, Babylonian *Yoma* 38a, Babylonian *Yevamot* 49b, Babylonian *Shabbat* 6a, etc.

30. Shem. Rabb. sec. Babylonia Gittin 60b, Rashi ad loc. See also Reuven Margolies, *Yesod Hamishnah Ve'arichatah,* 4th ed. (Jerusalem, 1955), p. 6 n. 4.

31. This was the reason that permission was found only with difficulty to commit the Oral Law to writing in the form of the

To have compiled such a list even for the use of teachers alone, a large number would have been necessary since elementary education was fairly general.[32] Such an undertaking must further have been rendered impossible, since it was even forbidden to commit the Shema, which received special attention in the curriculum of the schools, to writing.[33]

To consider that the teacher taught an oral list of 613 items to children of the ages of five to ten years[34] is ludicrous.[35] The instruction of small children in numerous details, difficult in themselves to remember, was obviated even in the period of the Geonim, when teaching of the prophetic books of the Bible commenced with Samuel because of the difficulty of assimilating the long lists of cities in Joshua.[36]

It is in any case hardly credible that a list used for teaching children could have assumed the importance of a recognized tradition in the hands of the Tannaim and their successors.

Professor M. Guttman also argues[37] in favor of the existence in writing of such a list. In reviewing the question as a whole, he says:

Mishnah. See I. Ginzberg, *Mishpatim Leisrael*: Harry Fischel Institute for Research, (Jerusalem, 1956), p. 49.

32. E. Ebner, *Elementary Education in Ancient Israel (10–220 C.E.)* (New York, 1956), p. 67.

33. Soferim 5:9. "One may not make the Shema and Hallel into separate scrolls for children. R. Judah permits it for the text of Genesis 1–5 and 1–8, but for all other books it is forbidden."

34. The age of elementary tuition in Bible, *Avot* 5:21.

35. Even for older students the Sifri, Ha'azinu, says, "In assimilating details one becomes weary, so that one does not know what to do." Cf. also the remarks of Nachmanides in Root One, on the laboriousness of the task of enumerating TaRYaG.

36. Assaph, *Tekupat Hageonim Vesiphrutat* (Jerusalem, 1954), p. 113 n. 9.

37. Bechinat HaMitzvot (Breslau, 1928), pp. 43 et seq.

The problem acquires a different perspective if we assume that not the number (TaRYaG) is the basis of our enquiry but a book or a tract. That some ancient well-known tract containing 613 subjects . . . with the object of summarizing part of the mitzvot of the Torah . . . existed.

The nature of this tract can now, of course, only be surmised, but it can be assumed that it was in the nature of a "bridge between Mikra and Mishnah." For, argues Guttman, it is difficult to see how students without previous introduction could leave the elementary school in which they were taught Mikra and immediately set about studying Mishnah and Talmud. Ergo, in practice this difficulty must have been overcome by instructing either orally or in writing in the content of Torah, by means of some compendium containing the essence of the Torah and its practical application. This compendium would also have served as a useful guide for those who did not enter the higher schools.

Guttman admits that this hypothesis is conjectural, but he attempts to draw proof from the nature of the Mishnah itself. This work avoids all elementary statement of the Torah law, which it assumes to be known to the student, who somehow must already have familiarized himself with the basic matter ignored in the Mishnah.

This theory is not unlike that previously referred to, and the difficulties already pointed out, in the way of assuming such a written tract to have been in existence, are not lessened by it. If the "tract" was a strictly oral affair, then, quite apart from the difficulty that the student must have experienced prior to entering the Mishnah school, because of the necessity to assimilate such a tract as a condition of entry, the argument in favor of a written tract largely defeats itself. But the theory is open to severe criticism on more fundamental grounds.

It is by no means certain that a "bridge" of the kind considered necessary by Guttman was indeed essential for one entering the Mishnah school. Children were taught reading and translation of the Bible in the elementary school. However, the translation was not always the literal one. But, bearing in mind the twofold aim of knowing the literal translation of the words and its authoritative interpretation for practical purposes, the official translation was also taught. This official translation "formed the bridge between Mikrah and Mishnah."[38] A boy entering the Mishnah school was not therefore unaware of the elementary base upon which the Mishnah is grounded.

In practice the conditions under which the Jew of the period lived provided ample illustration of the manner in which the laws of the Torah were to be translated into daily life, and it is not too much to assume that the student was acquainted by his manner of living with the normal requirements of the law.[39] For the Mishnah to commence[40] with a discussion of the *times* when the Shema was to be recited is perfectly normal when it is borne in mind that the student had been reciting the Shema since his earliest childhood.[41] A bridge in the sense of a wider guide to the precepts was unnecessary, since this was provided automatically by home, school, and environment.

---

38. Ebner, p. 80 and n. 33. Cf. also the remarks of Rabbenu Nissim in the *Sefer Hamafte'ach*.

39. Cf. Maimonides' commentary to *Menachot* 4:1.

40. *Berakhot* 1:1.

41. Sifre, Deuteronomy 46. "When the child knows to speak, his father must teach him Shema . . ."

To argue on a different plane, an appreciation of the Mishnah method of instruction fully illustrates the irrelevancy of such a bridge. The Mishnah was only committed to writing in its present form during the third century at the earliest, while prior to this momentous event the method of instruction in the Oral Law was the Midrash Halachah.[42] The very essence of this method implies study of the biblical text, to which rabbinic exegis was then applied. All that was required of the student was familiarity with the actual text of the Bible. Midrash Halachah itself took him through the succeeding stages.

After the compilation of the Mishnah it must not be assumed that radical changes in educational method came about.[43] The only basic change to take place was the replacement of the biblical text as the base for study by the standard Mishnah text. It was impossible to understand the Mishnah text, however, without the accompanying Midrash Halachah at the hands of a competent instructor. The Talmud itself affords ample evidence of the manner in which the study of the Mishnah was pursued.[44] The Mishnah was not treated as a textbook in isolation of its background or divorced from current rabbinic controversy. The

---

42. Sherira Gaon, in his famous letter, states that "in the earlier period of the Second Temple all the teachings of the Halachot were given in the manner in which they are found in our Sifra and Sifre." That is, in the Midrash form. See also Lauterbach, *Jewish Quarterly Review* (April 1915), p. 507 and n. 5 for further sources.

43. See the article by Lauterbach, ibid. pp. 508, et seq., and notes 8, 15, 22, and 53. He says, "At no time did the Mishnah for (i.e., the method of teaching the Halachah independently of the Written Law) become the exclusive method for teaching the Halachah, because the Midrash form never ceased to be in use."

44. Cf. Rashi, *Niddah* 7b. (bottom of page).

terse, somewhat cryptic language of the Mishnah necessi-
tated thorough, comprehensive examination if it was to be
comprehended. In the course of this examination all the
relevant matter would be considered as a matter of course. It
would in fact be entirely feasible for Mishnah study to have
taken place without even an elementary prior knowledge of
the biblical texts involved.[45] We are therefore confronted
with no difficulty of bridging Guttman's nonexistent gap
between Mikra and Mishnah. His conjecture, which is based
mainly on the existence of this gap, must therefore remain
largely hypothetical, and his attempt so to remove the problem of TaRYaG to the realm of history with a concrete formula
as its base falls largely to the ground. His strictures[46] upon
Maimonides and Nachmanides, who treat the problem in the
light of a received tradition, fall, in consequence, largely to
the ground.

Schechter, in quoting the dictum of R. Simlai,[47] is
inclined to the view that R. Simlai was interested in teaching a moral lesson to the public "without troubling himself
much about the accuracy of his numbers." This opinion, as
that of Bacher,[48] to the effect that R. Simlai is expressing a
moral lesson in symbolic terms, is also elaborated upon by
Moise Bloch.[49] If accepted, it renders the investigation into

---

45. Cf. Guttman's own remarks in "Die Anlehnung," Bericht des
Judische-theologischen Seminars (Breslau, 1924), p. 6—"whereas the
Written Law requires explanation, and its very existence in practice is
inconceivable without Midrash, the existence of the Oral Law is dependent upon itself, and the basis of its existence is completely independent of Midrash . . . with the Oral Law the Halachah comes before the
Bible. . . ."
46. *Bechinat HaMitzvot,* ibid.
47. *Some Aspects of Rabbinic Theology,* p. 138 et seq.
48. Terminology, Sect. 1, Tannaim, p. 80.
49. Revue d'Etudes Juives, 1, p. 208, quoted by Halper, ibid. Issa-

the silence of the Rabbis in the enumeration of TaRYaG meaningless, but this opinion is unfounded.

If R. Simlai had indeed been the originator of the "dogma" that the precepts of the Torah total 613, as Bloch assumes, a possible case could be made out for the polemical nature and understanding of the passage concerned.[50] But this is in fact far from the case.[51] As Halper correctly observes,[52] if R. Simlai were indeed the author of the tradition, at least some of the numerous references to TaRYaG should be introduced by the usual "kede'amar," as is customary throughout the Talmud when an original statement is being quoted.

This being so we are only able to accept the symbolic or polemical interpretation of the passage if we premise the fact that the symbolism is based upon an accepted, well-known tradition, and that the polemic is likewise based upon a fundamental Jewish truth. That this must be so is evidenced by the fact that throughout the Talmud[53] and the midrashim[54] the number is taken in its mathematical sense.

---

char Jacobson, *Chazon HaMikra* (Tel Aviv, 1956), pp. 408 et seq., also quotes Bloch's opinion with approval. He is mainly concerned with the polemical nature of the passage and fails to realize the inherent difficulties in Bloch's treatment of the subject. Cf. Weiss, ed., *Dor Dor VeDorshay,* vol. 3 (1923), p. 132.

50. But see here n. 7.

51. See chap. 3.

52. Ibid.

53. *Shabbat* 87a, *Yevamot* 47b, *Nedarim* 25a, *Shevu'ot* 29a, etc. In all of these instances the incidental manner in which the number TaRYaG is used is worthy of note. It but illustrates how deeply ingrained and taken for granted the tradition was during talmudic times. This could scarcely have been so if R. Simlai had been the originator of the tradition. See also chap. 3 n. 5.

54. Midrash Mishlei, 31. Midrash Tehillim, 17. Numbers Rabbah secs. 13 and 18. Exodus Rabbah 32. Shir Rabbah sec. 1. Tanchuma, Deuteronomy sec. Shofetim, Thetze. Pirkei D'R. Eliezer, chap. 41, etc.

The theories outlined above, two of which attempt to base the TaRYaG tradition in a historical background and the others in a symbolic setting, fail to withstand critical analysis. Does the traditional position of the handing down of TaRYaG from days of yore provide a suitable explanation for the failure of the Rabbis to provide satisfying treatment of a well-known, widely agreed upon tradition?[55] It would seem unlikely that the Scribes, who are credited with counting every letter of the Torah,[56] would consciously have ignored counting the number of precepts in the Torah. However, the appearance of the TaRYaG tradition in the early sources points to the fact that they did indeed enumerate the precepts.

The following passage in the Pesikhta[57] would seem to establish the fact that the talmudic teachers did indeed enumerate the mitzvot:

> Three sections Moses wrote in the Torah, each of which contains sixty mitzvot, they are the sections Pesachim, Nezikin, and Kedoshim; R. Levi in the name of R. Shilla said each contain seventy mitzvot. Said R. Tanchuma, they do not disagree, the one who considers the section on Pesachim to contain seventy mitzvot includes the section on Tefillin, the one who considers Nezikin to contain seventy, includes the section on Shemmittah, and the one who considers Kedoshim to contain seventy, includes the section on Ervah.[58]

---

55. The opinion of M. Bloch, p. 211, is completely without foundation, as shown at length by Guttman, *Bechinat Hamitzvot*, p. 29 et seq.

56. Babylonian *Kiddushin* 30a.

57. Hachodesh, 51:2.

58. The sections of Tefillin, Shemmittah, and Ervah immediately succeed the respective sections metioned.

The passage clearly illustrates that the Rabbis were acquainted even with the number of mitzvot contained in the individual sections of the Torah.[59] It cannot be far off the truth, therefore, to suggest that a complete list of TaRYaG was at their command.

The fact that a list containing their enumeration did not survive to the Tannaitic period is understandable if we bear in mind the reluctance to commit biblical extracts to writing.[60] That much was lost is evidenced by the fact that the talmudic teachers had to admit that even in counting the letters of the Torah "we are no longer expert."[61] It is not therefore surprising if, in the course of time, an oral list of TaRYaG failed, within the larger framework of the Oral Law itself, to be fully transmitted from generation to generation.

Scattered through the Tannaitic literature that has come down to us, one finds the statement "this is a positive precept" or "this is a prohibitive precept,"[62] which would in itself seem to indicate the remnant of such an orally transmitted enumeration of the precepts, which was called upon for the purpose of stressing particular biblical injunctions and their eligibility to be counted among a known number of positive or prohibitive precepts.

An acquaintance with the halachic literature of the Rabbis leaves one in no doubt of the fact that their purpose

---

59. See Mishnath R. Eliezer, section 15, where ten positive precepts and ten prohibitions are recorded in connection with the administration of justice. The ten prohibitions are enumerated in detail.

60. See also p. 7–8.

61. Babylonian *Kiddushin* 30a. On this problem see R. Margolith, "Hamikra Vehamassoret."

62. Sifre, Deuteronomy Pisk. 154, para. 3; ibid. Pisk. 157. para 4; ibid. Pisk. 203. para. 5; ibid. Pisk. 225, para. 1: Pisk. 227, para. 5; ibid. Pisk. 228, para. 1, etc.

and method were different from that of the present-day scholar, and although the modern scholar might deem it desirable for an important, far-reaching tradition such as this to be reduced to its fullest terms, the Rabbis may not have thought so. Their scientific outlook had a completely different color to that of the modern scholar and, while they enjoyed the fullest possible knowledge of the mitzvot of the Torah, it was of no moment in their eyes to submit a detailed list of TaRYaG to subsequent generations.

For the tradition to have had validity and currency in the earliest times, what was necessary was not a detailed list but an appreciation of the following major points, without which not even a hypothetical basis for TaRYaG is possible:

(a) that in connection with any mitzvah there must be differentiation between the essence of the mitzvah and its details as found in the Bible,

(b) that the implications of the mitzvah are not confused with the mitzvah itself, and

(c) that the received explanations of the mitzvah be not confused with the mitzvah itself.

That the Rabbis were fully aware of these points is evidenced throughout the Tannaitic literature.[63] Further, there is Tannaitic evidence for the classification of mitzvot in general terms and on varying bases,[64] which clearly

---

63. Sifra, chap. 18, para. 3, ibid. para. 6. sec. Behar, opening para. Bechukothai, paragraph 2. Sifre, Numbers, Pisk. 112. Deuteronomy Pisk. 2. Deuteronomy Pisk. 343, etc. Cf. also the statement in Exodus Rabbah chap. 32, "those who fulfill the 613 mitzvot *apart from the general rules, details, and implications.*"

64. See Sifra, Parsh. Chatt. paragraph 2, where a general division between idolatry and other mitzvot is made. In paragraph 6, a sixfold

illustrates the fact that the Rabbis were aware of the need for classification that TaRYaG entails.[65] The Mishnah itself groups series of related mitzvot together and numbers them. It is, however, important[66] to observe that for the most part the Mishnah groups the mitzvot under the headings of the punishments involved[67] and thereby resolves the problem of classification.

The aim of the Rabbis was the assimilation of a huge amount of material to terms in which it could be used in daily life, without interfering with the process of amplification and application.[68] For this purpose an enumeration of TaRYaG was irrelevant, since such a list could have little

---

classification according to the severity of punishment involved is made. Mechilt. De'Milluim, para. 23, lists a logical classification on the basis of generally similar features. Sifre, Numbers, Pisk. 111 gives a historical classification, while ibid. Pisk. 115 divides the mitzvot into those obligated upon members of both sexes and those only upon males. Sifre, Pisk. 44 classifies the mitzvot on the basis of those laws that apply irrespective of one's place of residence and those that apply only in the land of Israel. These examples by no means exhaust the list of classifications found in Tannaitic sources.

65. See here, p. 2–3.

66. See here, chap. 2.

67. *Sanhedrin* 7:4, by stoning, eighteen. Ibid. 9:1, by burning, nine. Ibid. by the sword, two. Ibid. 11:1, by strangling, seven. *Keritot* 1:1, by kareth, thirty-six. *Makkot* 3:1 the following receive corporal punishment. The Baraitha, *Sanhedrin* 83a, enumerates eleven transgressions for which the punishment is death at the hand of heaven. In *Menachot* 18b, the Baraitha lists all those mitzvot that pertain to the priest, a further indication of the natural grouping of precepts referred to in n. 64.

68. The need, in compiling a halachic code, to obviate interference with the *"process"* of Halachah, has dogged Jewish codifiers continually. The problem faced the compilers of the Mishnah and greatly influenced the shape of their product. It has been variously overcome by codifiers throughout the ages and is the fundamental reason for the striking diversity to be seen from code to code.

practical bearing. It would merely have stated briefly the biblical injunction or prohibition and would still have required to be related to

(a) the further relevant details as they appear in the Bible, and
(b) the received tradition concerning the particular texts involved.

The Rabbis, in using the method of Midrash Halachah, preferred to treat their subject matter as a whole since for practical purposes the details not included in a TaRYaG list are as relevant as TaRYaG themselves. Consequently, it was pointless to make too much of the actual member of TaRYaG. It was precisely the search for a fundamental base upon which to construct a compendium of Halachah and its ramifications that led Maimonides to his treatment of TaRYaG,[69] a search for which the Halachah itself has little need.

Seen therefore in its true relationship to Halachah as a whole, we may readily appreciate why the Rabbis did not provide a detailed enumeration of TaRYaG, and we may

---

69. See Maimonides' introduction to the S.H. In laying the ground plan for the *Mishneh Torah*, and following it through to its most brilliant conclusion, he ignored the *process* of Halachah. It was because of this that the code aroused so much criticism. It was felt that Maimonides' work tended toward the crystallization of Halachah at a particular stage of its development. Subsequent codifiers refused to follow in Maimonides' footsteps in their works. (Cf. previous note.) Halachah is in fact better off without a code in the strict sense of the word. It must be allowed freedom to develop and expand without the shackles imposed by an authoritative code. Halachah involves continual reexamination of principles, not reference to a textbook. See also chap. 6 n. 6 and 7.

readily understand why no lists of TaRYaG have come down to us from talmudic times.

In spite of what has been said above, it is nevertheless conceivable that such lists might indeed have existed, especially during the late talmudic period.

It will be shown below[70] that, contrary to accepted opinion, modern scholarship considers the work of the Halachot Gedolot not as the forerunner of TaRYaG lists but as being itself based upon a well-established tradition of TaRYaG enumerations. The earliest traceable lists indicate that enumerations of TaRYaG probably existed during the late Amoraic and Saboraic period. It is in any case difficult to credit the Rabbis with entirely ignoring the tradition and its implications.[71] One has but to open any work of the Rabbis to become apprised of the detailed care with which any theory affecting Halachah was carefully and even laboriously worked out. Surely this must have been so in connection with one of the most important traditions of all.

We have already shown that the groundwork for compiling such a detailed list was certainly at the command of the Rabbis and the important fact that for century after century the statements concerning TaRYaG were unchallenged during the talmudic period, something almost unique in Rabbinic literature, is itself an indication that the details of the tradition must have been known.

---

70. Chap. 4.
71. For the halachic implications, see chap. 2.

2

The Halachic Basis of TaRYaG

The lengthy argument in the previous chapter has been pursued from a particular standpoint concerning TaRYaG, namely, that the tradition in fixing the number of precepts at 613 does virtually nothing more than simply determine the number of precepts but has no practical value in Halachah. Although even in this context the historical and symbolical explanations of Guttman, Schechter, and Bacher have already been shown to be groundless, a major problem yet remains for the student of the TaRYaG literature.

Accepted that the number TaRYaG is to be taken in its arithmetical sense, given also the adequate reasons for the failure of the Rabbis of the Talmud to reduce the tradition to practical terms, why do so many masters of Halachah apply their keenest efforts to enumerating TaRYaG? What, ultimately, is the point of knowing whether there are TaRYaG mitzvot, or more or less?

Theologically, of course, it is of paramount importance to know the exact number of divine precepts, but
neither the Rabbis of the Talmud, who defined no definite
theological system, nor the post-talmudic masters of Halachah consider the problem from this point of view. Unless
Halachah itself is treated theologically, as well it might be,
this distinction finds few, if any, echoes in rabbinic works.

It has already been pointed out[1] that perhaps the most
important result of the TaRYaG literature is to be found in
the scientific analysis of Halachah to which it gave rise.
Halachah as a generic term for Jewish religious practice
needs to be broken down into its component parts, such as
biblical, rabbinic, custom, etc. This breaking down can be
achieved only by careful analysis of the entire corpus of
rabbinic literature. The fullest expression of halachic analysis to date is to be found in the TaRYaG literature. Careful
study of this literature, together with the cognate studies to
which it has given rise, clearly illustrates the importance of
the TaRYaG tradition. It will be shown below that clear
halachic distinction prevails between a member mitzvah
of TaRYaG and all other elements of Halachah.

It was to my mind the failure to discover any valid
reason for distinguishing the TaRYaG mitzvot that led Guttman and others to fanciful estimations of the origins of the
tradition. Their failure to examine TaRYaG from the standpoint of halachic principle was the reason for their inability
to appreciate the fundamental basis of TaRYaG.

In order to illustrate the halachic distinctions that
exist, it is necessary to consider Root Two of Maimonides'
Sefer HaMitzvot.

The root states:

---

1. See chap. 1 n. 26.

It is wrong to include in this number (TaRYaG) anything deduced by means of the thirteen hermeneutic
rules by which the Torah is expounded, or that
learned by means of an inclusion.

and Maimonides discusses it in the following manner:[2]

We have already explained in the Preface to the
Commentary on the Mishnah that most of the laws of
the Torah are deduced by means of the thirteen hermeneutic rules by means of which the Torah is to be
explained and that a law so deduced may sometimes
be the subject of controversy. There are (also) some
laws that are explanations received by tradition from
(the time of) Moses, in which, (while) there is no
controversy surrounding them, one of the rules is
adduced as its proof, because the possibility of discovering a hint of the explanation as traditionally received, or a comparison illustrating it, is inherent in
the Written Word. And we have fully explained this
matter there.

This being so, we need not declare concerning
every law deduced by the Sages by means of the rules
that it was "told to Moses at Sinai." We need not
assume also that everything found in the Talmud that
is based upon one of the rules is of rabbinic origin,
because occasionally the particular deduction is the
tradition received from Moses at Sinai. The correct
procedure is, therefore, that whatever is not explicitly
stated in the Torah but is found in the Talmud and
ascribed to deduction from one of the rules, *if they*

---

2. The translation is taken from my own unpublished translation
of the *Sefer HaMitzvot*.

themselves declare that it is of "the body of the Torah,"
or of biblical origin, it ought to be included (in TaRYaG)
since the receivers of tradition declare it to be biblical.
If they do not declare it to be so, and they make no
mention of it(s biblical origin), it is not taught by any
verse and is of rabbinic origin.[3]

This is also one of the Roots in which others have
erred, because of this he[4] has included "fearing the
wise" among the positive precepts. It seems to me
that what led him to this (inclusion) is the comment (to
the verse) "Thou shalt fear the Lord thy God,"[5] on
which R. Akiba says,[6] "this includes (the fear of) the
wise." He considered that anything learned by means
of the thirteen rules is of the aforementioned general
rule. But if it is indeed as they think, why did they not
include the respect due to a stepfather and a stepmother as separate mitzvot linked with honoring parents, as also the respect due to an elder brother? For
that we must honor these persons we learn from an
"inclusion," as the Talmud says,[7] "Honor thy father,"[8]
this includes your elder brother; and they said "thy
father" (Hebrew "eth" avicha), this includes a stepfather, and "thy mother" (Hebrew "eth" imecha), includes a stepmother, in the same manner that they
declared "fear the (Hebrew eth) Lord thy God," includes (fearing) the wise. Why then did they include

---

3. My italics.
4. The author of the *Halachot Gedolot*, against whom most of
Maimonides' criticisms are directed. See chap. 5.
5. Deuteronomy 10:20.
6. *Pesachim* 22b.
7. *Ketubot* 103a.
8. Exodus 20:12.

some and not others? And in this foolishness they have gone even further in the following instance. On discovering that an exposition of a verse obligates certain actions, or distances particular matters, cases that are certainly rabbinic, they have included them in their list of mitzvot, in spite of the fact that the literal sense of the verse indicates none of these matters.

The Sages, of blessed memory, have already enlightened us by stating,[9] *"A verse does not lose its literal meaning," and we continually find the Talmud asking "what is the literal rendering of the verse?"* (even) *when deducing from it diverse meanings and proofs.*[10] "And those relying on this opinion have enumerated in their list of mitzvot, "visiting the sick," "comforting the mourners," and "burying the dead" because of the exposition of the verse,[11] "And thou shalt make known to them the way in which they should walk, and the deed that they shall do," in which they state,[12] "the way"—this refers to acts of charity; "they should walk,"—this refers to visiting the sick; "in which"—this refers to burying the dead; "and the deed"—this refers to the laws; "that they shall do"—this refers to doing more than the letter of the law requires. They consider each of these actions as a separate mitzvah, not realizing that all of these deeds, and others similar to them, are included under one of the explicit mitzvot of the Torah, namely, when He of Blessed Memory declares, "Thou shalt love thy neighbor as thyself.[13]

---

9. *Shabbat* 63a.
10. My italics.
11. Exodus 18:20.
12. *Bava Kamma* 100a.
13. Leviticus 19:18.

Similarly they have included "reckoning the seasons," as a separate mitzvah because of the exposition of the verse,[14] "for it is your wisdom and understanding in the eyes of the Peoples," in which they say, "What is the wisdom and understanding that is in the sight of the Peoples? This is the reckoning of the seasons and planetary movements."[15]

If he had have listed that which is more clearly expressed than this, and he had have enumerated that which it is more fitting to list, namely, everything learned from the Torah by means of one of the rules by which the Torah is expounded, the number of mitzvot would total many thousands.

You may perhaps think that I refrain from including them because I think them untrue! But, whether the law, deduced by means of a particular rule, be true or false is not the (criterion of inclusion or exclusion). The reason (for excluding them lies in the fact) that everything deduced by a person, be the person even Moses himself, is as shoots from the roots that are the 613 mitzvot told to Moses explicitly at Sinai, and may not therefore be included.[16] Proof of which lies in the talmudic statement[17] that "the seventeen hundred minor and major (cases of deduction), comparisons, and laws deduced by the Scribes, which were forgotten during the period of mourning for Moses, were restored by the acumen of Othniel ben Kenaz, as it is written,[18] "whosoever will smite Kiryat Sefer and cap-

---

14. Deuteronomy 4:6.
15. *Shabbat* 75a.
16. My italics.
17. *Temurah* 16a.
18. Joshua 15:16.

ture it . . . and Othniel ben Kenaz captured it." But if such was the number of forgotten (laws), how many must the total have been for this number to be forgotten from it!—for it is obviously false to say that everything known was forgotten. It is therefore without any doubt that the laws that had been deduced by means of the minor and major and other rules totaled many thousands, all of which were known at the time of Moses and were termed, "laws deduced by the Scribes (Divrei Soferim)." *For whatsoever was not heard explicitly from Sinai is called "the words of the Scribes."*[19]

It is therefore clear that (among) the 613 mitzvot that were told to Moses at Sinai must not be included anything learned by means of the thirteen rules, even (if it was learned) in his (own) time, of blessed memory, and certainly not that which was learned subsequently. Nevertheless one may include that which was explicitly received from him, namely, that when the transmitters (of the Law) declare concerning a prohibition that it is biblical, or if they say it is of "the body of the Torah," (then) it may be counted, for *it is known by tradition and not by logical deduction;*[20] the mention of logical deduction and proof in its connection being merely to illustrate the inherent wisdom of the Written Word, as we have explained in the commentary to the Mishnah.

The plain meaning of Maimonides' statement is apparently diametrically opposed to the sense of the Talmud. Whereas the latter seems, on almost every one of its pages,

19. My italics.
20. My italics. See chap. 7 n. 29.

to uphold the view that a law deduced by means of one of the hermeneutic rules is of biblical standing and authority, Maimonides states that unless a contrary view is expressed by the talmudic authorities, a law so deduced is to be considered as rabbinic only.

Nachmanides, holding with the plain sense of the Talmud, opposes this view and declares that every law deduced by means of the rules is of biblical standing unless the Talmud itself states that the verse is simply an "Asmakhtah,"[21] in which case it is only of rabbinic authority. Nachmanides concludes his comments on Root Two with the words,

> For this Book of the Master, of Blessed Memory, is sweet and full of delight, except for this Root in which He tears apart great mountains in the Talmud and throws down fortified walls in the Gemara. For students of the Gemara it is evil and bitter. Let it be forgotten and not discussed.

Indeed, this is the only instance in Nachmanides' manifold halachic writings in which he indulges in personal criticism of Maimonides, and the reason is quite clear. Maimonides is considered to be impinging upon the sanctity and authority of the Oral Law.

The fact that Maimonides considers all Halachot deduced by means of the rules in a manner differing from the "Shittat Ha-Talmud" gave rise to an extremely interesting historical development.

---

21. Asmakhtah.—An interpretation of a verse that does not represent the actual meaning of the verse. The explanation or law is simply pegged to the verse to facilitate the memory. See *Encyclopedia Talmudit*, vol. 2, pp. 105–108. But in N. B. Ritva to R. H. 16a, s.q. Tanya.

Instead of accepting Maimonides' singular view and discarding it in practice, owing to the weight of contrary talmudic authority and halachic precedent,[22] attempts were made to "interpret" his opinion. Scholars felt that it was simply impossible for Maimonides to disagree with the Talmud on so fundamental an issue, which, in practical Halachah, has repercussions in every sphere of religious practice. This "interpretation" was further felt to be imperative in view of the fact that Maimonides in his Yad Hachazakkah seemed to have ignored the principles that he himself had set out in Root Two of his *Sefer HaMitzvot*.

It came to be held[23] by most authorities that Nachmanides had misunderstood Root Two and that in reality Maimonides' opinion was that laws deduced by means of the rules were to be considered rabbinic only in so far as their inclusion in the TaRYaG list was concerned, since they were not explicitly stated in the Torah, although the actual laws themselves enjoyed biblical status and authority. Many of those who upheld his interpretation of Maimonides' words differed in particular instances among themselves, and great acumen is displayed in the attempt to reconcile various Maimonist dicta along these more conventional lines. The

---

22. The attempts by various scholars to equate Maimonides' stand with certain of his predecessors, notably with the teachers of Rashi, as quoted by Rashi to *Ketubot* 3a, is shown to be mistaken by Neubauer, pp. 4–17.

23. R. Shimeon b. R. Zemach Duran was the first to reinterpret Maimonides in this manner. He says, (*Zohar HaRakia*, Root Two), "And many years have passed, during which the true understanding of our teacher was not revealed, and in our humble opinion there was revealed unto us that which was not revealed unto them." However, Ra'abad (Ishuth, end chap. 3), Addereth (resp. pr. II, no. 230), Ribash (resp. 163), and others, including the author of the Chinuch (precept 282, etc.) understand Maimonides as Nachmanides understood him.

terminology of Maimonides is taken as the base for this trend of interpretation.

Three main divisions of laws thus came into existence:

1. Deoraitha—the actual laws stated in the text of the Torah
2. Divrei Soferim—laws deduced by means of the rules, and
3. Derabbanan—laws of completely rabbinic origin

This is not the place to treat of these categories at length, but it must be noted that while according to this opinion the second category, Divrei Soferim, enjoy biblical status, they are not actually to be equated with the laws stated in the Torah, the Deoraitha. They enjoy a kind of intermediate status, between the Deoraitha and the Derabbanan. They are forbidden by the Torah but carry with them no biblical penalty and are termed "Issura Bealma."[24]

None of the hermeneutic rules of Halachah may be used to interpret them,[25] and the Rabbis make no fence around laws of this category.[26] Preference is given to an

---

24. See Peri Megadim, *Pessicha Kolelet, Orach Chayyim* (Warsaw, 1877), sect. 1, para. 2. See also *Mitzvot Hashem* (Frankfurt, 1857), p. 108, Klal 17, "The punishment for any rabbinic matter is Makkath Marduth. Likewise for anything not explicitly stated in the Torah, even if learned by means of one of the rules by which the Torah is explained, the punishment is Makkat Mardut." (Makkat Mardut is the term used for the infliction of corporal punishment enjoined by the Rabbis.)

25. *Shabbat* 132a, and Rashi ad loc. para. Akiba Cf. also Yadayim, chap. 3, mishnah 2. See also, Sefer Hakkrithut, pt. I, sec. 11, where it is stated that Divrei Soferim may not be deduced from Divrei Soferim, nor from the Deoraitha. Cf. Rabbenu Asher to *Niddah* 7b.

26. Peri Megadim, pt. 3 n. 1.

explicitly stated law over one of this class,[27] and according to Maimonides,[28] a law deduced by the Beth Din Hagadol by means of one of the rules can be repealed by a later Beth Din Hagadol.[29] The law governing the rebellious elder[30] applies only to matters not explicitly stated in the Torah, that is, cases under this heading,[31] while the expiatory offering brought by the whole congregation[32] for an error in their rendering of a legal decision applies only to an instance with which the Saduccees are not in agreement.[33] Now the Saduccees agreed with what was explicitly stated in the Torah but not with that which was deduced by means of the rules. Likewise the prohibition against deciding a law (Hora'ah) while in a state of drunkenness[34] does not apply to that which is explicitly stated in the Torah.[35]

According to Maimonides in Root One, any infringement of a law deduced by means of the rules involves one in transgression of both a positive and prohibitive commandment.[36] There are a number of other differences

---

27. Ibid. n. 2.

28. Mamrim, chap. 2, *Challah* 1.

29. This does not, however, apply in the case of Takkanot or Seyyagim unless certain conditions are present, ibid.

30. Deuteronomy 17:12.

31. See Commentary of Maimonides to *Sanhedrin*, chap. 11, mishnah 2, and Yad, Mamrim, chap. 3, *Challah* 1.

32. Leviticus 4:13–21.

33. *Horayot*, 4a.

34. *Eruvin* 64b. S.H. Prohibition 73. Cf. also Semak 133.

35. *Keritot* 13b. Torah Kohanim, Shemini, end Parsha Aleph, and Commentary of Ra'abad, ad loc. n. 9. Yad, Baith Mikdash, chap. 1, *Challah* 3. The term *Horaah* in fact applies only to the Oral Law, as is obvious from these sources and nn. 31 to 33.

36. Deuteronomy 17:11. In Root One Maimonides says:
   because everything that the Sages enjoined upon us, and all

between laws classed as Deoraitha and laws classed as
Divrei Soferim scattered throughout rabbinic literature,[37]
but the instances already mentioned suffice for our present
purpose. Whether we accept Maimonides' view as it stands
and as Nachmanides understands it, and consider all laws
deduced by means of the rules as rabbinic,[38] or whether we

---

that they warned us against, was upheld by Moses our teacher at
Sinai when he said, "By the word of the law that they shall teach
you . . ."

and He, of blessed memory, warned us against infraction of
anything the Sages enacted or decreed, by the words:

"thou shalt not turn aside. . . ."

See also S.H. positive commandment 174. Prohibition 312. Saadya
Gaon's list is the only one that omits these two precepts. Possibly the
reason is that Saadya considers them to embrace the entire Torah—as a
precondition for the acceptance of the obligation toward fulfillment of
the precepts. For a similar reason Behag omits the precept to believe in
God. See chap. 5 n. 35.

37. See *Yadayim Shevu'ot* chap. 5 *Challah* 2; *Yadayim* Shechitah,
chap. 5, *Challah* 3. Yoreh Deah, 239, para. 6. Minchat Chinuch, Mitzvah, 498; Kinass Soferim to Root Two; Peri Megadim, pt. 3 n. 2; ibid. pt.
4 n. 12, etc. Sede Chemed, ed. Warsaw, vol. 4, Maarechet HaKlallim,
Dalet, no. 5; ibid. pt. 14; no. 64; ibid. pt. 15, no. 135; ibid. pt. 16, no. 26;
etc. *Encyclopedia Talmudit*, vol. 7, p. 101. Rabbenu Asher to Betza,
beginning of chap. 4, and Rema to *Or Hachayyim*, 605, para. 2.

38. Maimonides, in considering these laws as rabbinic, does hold
definite views on the gradation of various types of laws deduced. For
example, where the Rabbis state the law to be biblical, it is so even if
deduced by means of the rules. Where the Rabbis use the rules to
interpret biblical statements, the result is as if written in the Torah.
Where the Rabbis state that they have received "MiPI Ha'Shemuah,"
the law is biblical, and so on. Thus the actual number of instances
where difference appertains between Maimonides and Nachmanides
is greatly reduced. In any event, the remarks in Root Two can only be
fully understood by carefully examining all of the places where he
discusses the matter, his preface to the Mishnah and commentary
thereon, his responsa as well as the *Yadayim* must be thoroughly
studied before a true estimate of his opinion can be formed. The most
thorough and painstaking treatment of Maimonides on these lines is to

accept the interpretation of his words as offered by Duran and adhered to by subsequent scholars, it is abundantly clear that halachic distinction certainly exists between a law stated explicitly in the Torah, that is, a member of TaRYaG, and all other laws, however made known. Consequently it is beyond doubt that the problem of TaRYaG is a halachic and not a historical problem.

Even according to Nachmanides, who considers laws deduced by means of the rules as absolutely biblical, distinction in most of the points mentioned above exists.[39] In addition, a most fundamental distinction is to be found in the fact that no biblical punishment applies in the case of a law learned by means of the rules, except in the case of "Gezera Shave" and "Hekesh."[40] The two exceptions are due to the fact that anything learned by their means is considered as if explicitly stated in the verse.[41] It is

---

be found in the commentary Lev Sameach, by R. Abraham Allegri, first printed Constantinople, 1652, and subsequently in most editions of the S.H.

39. The distinction drawn by R. G. Mendel, author of *Machshevet Moshe*, commentary to the S.H. (Vilna, 1865), p. 31, is not at all convincing.

40. Peri Megadim, pt. 1 n. 11.

41. Maimonides also agrees with this when the law learned is in agreement with one of the conditions making it Deoraitha. Therefore, although "betrothal by means of money" is termed by him Divrei Soferim (Ishuth. chap. 1 *Challah* 2. But see Melechet Shlomo to *Kiddushin* 1:1, who quotes the testimony of Maimonides' son to the effect that Maimonides corrected his own copy of this passage to read that such betrothal is "Deoraitha"), one who cohabits with a woman betrothed by this means is liable to capital punishment as an adulterer because in this instance the Rabbis are simply explaining the biblical verse of betrothal (Deuteronomy 24:1), see *Kiddushin* 2a. See also S.H. Prohibitions 132, 135. See also Rashi to *Pesachim* 24a. *Sukkah* 11b. *Niddah* 19b; Chiddushei HaRaN to *Sanhedrin* 43. RaSHBAH and Nachmanides to *Bava Metzia* 87b. etc., to the effect that no one may

abundantly clear, therefore, that even according to Nachmanides, the problem of TaRYaG indeed has its basis in
Halachah.

According to some authorities,[42] the reason for the
repetition by the Torah of the verses, "thou shalt not
add,"[43] and "thou shalt not diminish,"[44] is in order to
teach that no mitzvah may be added to or subtracted
from the TaRYaG mitzvot of the Torah. Such addition or
subtraction involves one in transgression of the biblical
law not to diminish or to add. Clear knowledge of TaRYaG
is consequently essential in order to avoid transgressing
one of these two injunctions.[45] In addition, according to

---

invent a Gezera Shave. It may only be used if handed down from
teacher to teacher from the time of Moses. See the discussion in J. Z.
Mecklenberg, *Haketav Vehakabala* (New York: On Publishing, 1946),
pp. XII ff. See also the comments of Gersonides on the Thirteen Rules,
published in *Sinai* 47:no. 8 (May 1960): 85. CF. also the remarks of the
Chinuch, precept 154 in connection with the prohibition concerning
unclean beasts, which is drawn from a Kal Vachomer. Likewise some
mandates are drawn from a Kal Vachomer (inference a fortiori), but the
Kal Vachomer is considered only as rendering a known law explicit—
"Gilui Miltha Be'alma"—hence the law so derived incurs biblical punishment as if stated explicitly in the Torah. See Yad, Tum'at Meth 1, 2 for
three such examples.

42. See *Encyclopedia Talmudit*, vol. 3, pp. 326, 330. Also, commentary of Professor D. Z. Hoffman to Deuteronomy 4:2 and Nachmanides
ad loc. From Maimonides' remarks at the end of the preface to *Mishneh
Torah*, it seems he was also of this opinion. For he says, "And against
what did the Torah warn, "Thou shalt not add to it, and shalt not
diminish from it," that no prophet may invent a new matter and say,
the Holy One blessed be He, commanded him to add this to the
precepts of the Torah or to remove one of these 613 precepts." Cf. also
Yesodei Hatorah, chap. 9, *Challah* 1.

43. Deuteronomy 4:2 and 13:1.

44. Ibid.

45. See *Yadayim Mamrim* 2:9, where Maimonides codifies the
prohibition restricting the Beth Din Hagadol from promulgating ordinances and decrees if they were mitzvot of the Torah.

Rashba[46] and others, failure to perform a positive commandment involves one in the prohibition "not to diminish." It is therefore essential to differentiate the 248 positive commandments.

---

46. See Minchat Chinuch to precept 455.

3

The Early Sources

The opinion has been expressed[1] that the entire concept of TaRYaG was unknown during the Tannaitic period. According to this view the origin of TaRYaG is to be discovered in the saying of the third-century Amora R. Simlai,[2] and has no Tannaitic antecedents. Mention has already been made[3] of Halper's pointed argument against the ascription of the founding of the tradition to this teacher. In addition to Halper's argument, extant Tannaitic texts themselves illustrate that the number TaRYaG was known and accepted during the Tannaitic period. A study of these

---

1. Middot Soferim Weiss on Mechilta Bachodesh, sec. 5 n. 50 (Vienna, 1856). I. S. Hurwitz, *Yad Halevi*, pt. 1, pp. 113–115. R. Menachem Azariah in a responsum quoted by Hurwitz, p. 115. Ginsberg, *Legends of the Jews*, vol. 6, p. 31 n. 181.
2. Quoted fully at the beginning of chapter 1.
3. Chap. 1.

texts also throws interesting light on the question of when in fact TaRYaG gained actual currency.[4]

It is in any case difficult to assume that had R. Simlai indeed been the author of the tradition, his statement would not only have remained unchallenged but would have been assimilated by teachers of the eminence of R. Yohannan and R. Yehoshua ben Levi,[5] his renowned contemporaries.

For a teaching of this nature to gain immediate acceptance, it must already have enjoyed currency for some considerable time. The tacit acceptance of R. Simlai's statement proves that this was so, so that even without direct Tannaitic reference, one would be justified in assuming some Tannaitic currency of the tradition.

Three[6] Tannaitic passages that feature the number TaRYaG exist in the Tannaitic literature that has come down to us.

---

4. See below, this chapter.

5. R. Yohannan was a pupil of R. Judah the Prince. He sat in the Beth Hamidrash of the Tannaim and records much of the teaching of the Tannaim R. Shimeon ben Elazar, R. Elazar ben R. Shimeon, and R. Eliezer ben R. Jose the Galilian. His use of TaRYaG is quoted by Bacher, Agg. Am. vol. 1, pt. 2, and ibid., p. 97. R. Yehoshua ben Levi was one of the most renowned of the third-century Amoraim. He was related by marriage to R. Judah the Prince and Bar Kappara. His statement on TaRYaG is recorded in Shir. Rabb., chap. 1. These two teachers enjoy a status that is a little difficult to determine exactly. In common with their contemporary, Rab, who also studied at the feet of the Tannaim, they may be said to enjoy, as did Rab, the status of semi-Tanna, or Tanna–Amora, see Tosafot to *Ketubot* 8a, and Rashi to *Niddah* 26a. On the subject of Tanna–Amora see M. Fogelman in *Sinai* 21:1 (October 1957): 25–30. They would certainly not use a tradition formulated by a lesser contemporary, in the unquestioned, incidental manner in which they do, unless they had received it from their own teachers.

6. Halper, *Jewish Quarterly Review*, and Guttman, *Bechinat HaMitzvot*, are in fact only aware of two Tannaitic sources.

The following passage occurs in the Mechilta:[7]

> Said R. Shimeon ben Elazar, if the seven precepts that
> the sons of Noah were commanded and that they
> accepted upon themselves, they are unable to ob-
> serve fully,[8] how much more certain would their fail-
> ure be with all the precepts of the Torah. This is to be
> compared to a king who appointed two guardians,
> one over a storehouse of straw and the other over a
> storehouse of silver and gold. The appointee over the
> one of straw was suspected of dishonesty but he
> complained because he was not set over the store-
> house of silver and gold. The one who had been
> appointed over the storehouse of silver and gold said
> to him, "Empty head, if you falsified the trust placed
> in you in the case of straw, how much more so would
> you have done in the case of the silver and gold." If
> the sons of Noah could not fulfill seven precepts, how
> much less would they have been able to fulfill 613.

Weiss[9] and Guttman[10] doubt the authenticity of the passage
and consider the number 613 to be an interpolation, the
former because he is unaware that the Tannaim had a
number for the precepts, the latter owing to various readings of the text that have been preserved. However, the
fact that Weiss was unaware of the use by the Tannaim of
the number TaRYaG is far from being a convincing argument, especially in view of the fact that two predecessors
of R. Shimeon ben Elazar, namely, Ben Azzai and R.

---

7. Bachodesh, sec. 5.
8. Literally, stand by them.
9. Middot Soferim to this passage.
10. *Bechinat HaMitzvot*, p. 28.

Eliezer ben R. Jose Hagalilli, indeed do use the number.[11]
An indication that R. Shimeon ben Elazar did in fact
number the mitzvot is found in the following passage from
the Aboth D'R. Nathan:[12]

> R. Shimeon ben Elazar . . . moreover let them be dis-
> tinctly marked from one another and let them be
> distinctly marked one beside the other

on which Goldin remarks that the meaning of this obscure
passage seems to be

> that the contents of the Torah ought to be classified
> into groups and then the groups logically related to
> one another.

This, however, would obviously entail some numbering of
the contents of the Torah. The evidence that R. Shimeon
ben Elazar did in fact number, or was at least acquainted
with the number of the precepts, is to be found in the
above-quoted passage from the Mechilta.

The following passage occurs in the Sifri:[13]

---

11. See above.
12. Golding, p. 102 and n. 12.
13. Ed. Ish Shalom (New York, 1948). Deuteronomy Piska 76. In the
Koleditzky edition (Jerusalem, 1948) (this edition is based on the
manuscripts of the medieval scholar Rabbenu Hillel, and Ben Zera
Abraham), the note by Koleditzky, Anaf 93, should obviously read
"and sixty-four" not "and sixty-five." The reading in Malbim's edition
of the Sifri (Vilna, 1890) is very difficult to establish since according to
Malbim one must read "Shalosh Mitzvot Assah" and not "Mitzvot
Asseh."

R. Shimeon ben Azzai says, there are 365 prohibitions
in the Torah, and no such statement is made about any
of them . . .

This passage is certainly a Tannaitic source of the first
importance, since even the exact number[14] of prohibitions
is recorded.

D. Z. Hoffman discovered a further reading of Ben
Azzai's statement in the Midrash Haggadol to Deuteron-
omy, which he incorporated in his Midrash HaTannaim.[15]
The reading is:

Said Ben Azzai, there are 300 Mitzvot Asseh as
this . . .

The reading is difficult because Ben Azzai is dealing
with a prohibition and not a positive commandment;
but if the reading in this respect is mistaken, there remains proof from the passage that Ben Azzai listed the
commandments.

The number 300 fits neither the accepted total of
positive nor prohibitive precepts but is not to be discarded[16] for this reason. It is, of course, possible that the
Tanna is merely using the number three hundred in the
sense of a round number.[17] But, assuming that he is being

---

14. And not as C. B. Chavell, *The Book of Divine Commandments*
(Soncino Press, 1940), Foreword, p. xvi, who, while not ascribing
authorship of the TaRYaG tradition to R. Simlai, does ascribe to him the
division of the precepts into 248 positive commandments and 365
prohibitions.

15. Edited and published by Hoffman in 1908–1909. This midrash is
a combination of our Sifri and the lost Mechilta of R. Ishmael to
Deuteronomy.

16. As does Ginzberg, *Legends*, vol. 6, p. 31 n. 181.

17. Cf. Rabbenu Asher to *Pesachim* ch. 10, Sim. 40.

exact, this would allow for the conjecture that there may have existed more than one method of listing the precepts and that the division into 248 and 365 represents only one tradition of several.[18] If this were indeed so, it would alleviate the pressing problem of trying to fit the precepts of the Torah into the accepted divisions. To date, no enumeration has been entirely successful[19] but, if the field were opened to other combinations of positive and prohibitive precepts, a definitive list might eventually be forthcoming.

The following passage occurs in the Midrash Haggadol to Genesis:[20]

> Said R. Eliezer ben R. Jose the Galilian, "Where does the Torah state the reward for the righteous? As it is written,[21] 'Thy reward is very great,' from which we may infer that if in the case of Abraham our father, who was not enjoined to observe the fine details of Torah, it is written, thy reward is very great, one who fulfills 613 mitzvot how much more so . . ."

18. Cf. also Zohar HaRakia, end.

19. See chap. 1, pp. 6 and 7.

20. Ed. Mordechai Margolies (Jerusalem, 1947), p. 244. The source of this passage is Mishnah R. Eliezer sec. 3, p. 54, ed. by H. G. Enelow (New York: Bloch, 1933). The editor is of the opinion that the work is pretalmudic. On the Mishnath R. E. see J. N. Epstein, in H.U.C.A. 1950–1951, Hebrew sec. p. 10. Both Saadya Gaon and Maimonides (pos. comm. no. 5, in S.H.) quote the Mishnah R. Eliezer. A further passage from this work, p. 372, is quoted by Midrash Haggadol, Exodus, ed. M. Margolies (Jerusalem, 1956), p. 674. It reads: "Great is the Sabbath, for the Torah provided it as a test to judge who is a righteous proselyte, for it enumerates of the 613 mitzvot only the Sabbath. . . ." Although this passage may also be Tannaitic, according to Enelow's supposition, since it is prefaced by no superscription it must remain doubtful.

21. Genesis 15:1.

All of the manuscripts of the Midrash Haggadol agree in this quotation so that we have here a third source amongst the pupils of R. Akiba using the number TaRYaG. These three passages are the earliest recorded mentionings of the tradition.[22]

The authorities using the number are the Tannaim, Ben Azzai,[23] R. Eliezer ben R. Jose the Galilian,[24] and R. Shimeon Ben Elazar.[25] It is not without great significance for our enquiry that these three Tannaim are all of the school of R. Akiba. It is likely that the statement concerning TaRYaG in Exodus Rabbah[26] is a continuation of the words of R. Nehemiah—since the statement explains his words. Since he was also a pupil of R. Akiba, we have a fourth Tanna of this school familiar with the number TaRYaG. It might therefore well be that the school of R. Akiba, which was so intensely occupied with the classification of the Oral Law, is responsible also for the number TaRYaG in connection with the commandments contained in the written law. However, this reasoning can only be accepted

---

22. In view of the dating of the Targum Jonathan by Zunz, the passage in this Targum, on Exodus 24:12, cannot be considered. There are, however, serious objections to Zunz's dating of this Targum in his *Sermons of Israel*, ed. Albeck (Jerusalem, 1947), chap. 5. Harkavy in his Geonic Responsa, nos. 15 and 248, prints a responsum of R. Sherira Gaon, who states that the Targum Jonathan was well known to the Amoraim. See also *Otzar Hageonim*, ed. B. M. Levin (Jerusalem, 1932), vol. 5, to *Megillah* 3b.

23. Ben Azzai was both a Talmid and a chaver of R. Akiba. They apparently studied under the same teacher, R. Yehoshua ben Chananiya. See Bacher Agg. HaTTan, vol. 1, pt. 2, no. 15.

24. R. Eliezer ben R. Jose was a pupil of R. Akiba and renowned in the field of Aggadah. See Bacher, vol. 2, pt. 2, chap. 8.

25. R. Shimeon ben Elazar was a pupil of R. Meir, the pupil of R. Akiba. See, Frankel, Darchei HaMishnah (1923), p. 211.

26. Chap. 32.

with an important qualification. It has been shown in the previous chapter that TaRYaG carries definite halachic status, and it is certainly too much to assume that sight of this halachic status was lost until the time of R. Akiba and his school, especially so in view of the fact that many of the halachic qualities of TaRYaG[27] had ceased to be operative[28] in the time of R. Akiba. It must therefore be concluded that the halachic differences of those mitzvot that came later to be known as TaRYaG were well known, but the actual number TaRYaG only became crystallized during the activity of the school of R. Akiba.

There is, however, one indication that the number TaRYaG may antedate even this period.

Various talmudic[29] and midrashic[30] sources take for granted two traditions concerning the precepts.[31] These traditions are, one, that of grouping the precepts of the Torah under the headings of the Decalogue, and two, the number TaRYaG. These traditions are intertwined. The idea of grouping the precepts under the headings of the Decalogue is at least as old as Philo.[32] The Midrash[33] points out that the 620 letters in the Decalogue refer to TaRYaG mitzvot, the remaining seven being variously ascribed to

---

27. See chap. 2.

28. The law governing a rebellious elder applies only when the Sanhedrin is sitting in session in the Hewn Chamber of the Temple. *Sanhedrin* 14b. *Yadayim* Mamrim, chap. 3, *Challah* 5. The law governing the "offering by the Congregation" (Levi 4:13–21), see requote chap. 2, obviously applies only while the Temple is in existence.

29. *Yevamot* 47b, *Shabbat* 87a, and Rashi ad loc. Jerusalem *Shekalim*, chap. 6, *Challah* 1. Jerusalem *Sotah*, chap. 8, *Challah* 3.

30. Aboth D'R. Nathan, ed. Golding, Yale Judaica, vol. 10, p. 21 and n. 30. *Bamidbar Rabbah* chaps. 13 and 18.

31. On this subject, see chap. 4.

32. Philo, De Special Leg. also on the Decalogue, 29.

33. *Bamidbar Rabbah*, chap. 18.

either the seven Naochide laws or the seven rabbinic laws.[34] But if the TaRYaG tradition is indeed a later tradition, why was the anomaly of 613 precepts for 620 letters left? It would have been a simple matter to declare that not 613 but 620 mitzvot are in the Torah.[35] That this was not done would seem to indicate that the number TaRYaG is coterminal with, if not earlier than, the idea of grouping the mitzvot under the Decalogue.[36]

In addition to the Tannaim mentioned there are several Amoraim who use the number TaRYaG[37] and many anonymous references scattered throughout rabbinic literature.[38]

---

34. See the interesting remarks in Peri Megadim, General Introduction to *Or Hachayim*, para 1.

35. *Bamidbar Rabbah*, chap. 21, stresses the difference between the number of letters in the Decalogue and the number TaRYaG.

36. It is, however, possible that the arrangement of taking the letters of the Decalogue to represent the mitzvot is of later origin.

37. R. Yohannan, R. Yehoshua ben Levi (see here chap. 2). R. Hamnuna, *Makkot* 23b. R. Eliezer ben Pedat, *Yevamot* 47b. R. Yehuda ben R. Simon, *Genesis Rabbah* chap. 24. Shir. *Rabbah*, chap. 1. R. Abba, see Tanchuma, Thetze. R. Acha n. 5.

38. *Shabbat* 87a; *Nedarim* 25a; *Shevu'ot* 29a; *Exodus Rabbah*, chap. 32; *Bamidbar Rabbah*, chaps. 13 and 18. Shir. *Rabbah*, chap. 1. Midrash Mishlei, 31. Midrash Tehillim 17. Mishnath R. Eliezer n. 19. Pirkei D'R. Eliezer, chap. 41. Several additional references are to be found in Ginzberg, *Legends*, vol. 1, p. 379 (cf. Rashi to Genesis 32:5); vol. 3, pp. 96, 441, and 469.

4

The Azharot

I

Jewish tradition has asserted and upheld from the very earliest times that the Pentateuch is but the amplification of the Decalogue, which, if rightly understood, embraces the entire legal system of the Torah. The relationship between Decalogue and Pentateuch is that of the general rule to the detail.[1] This approach to the Decalogue is not a fancy of the Rabbis; it is axiomatic and lies at the very core of traditional Jewish thought: that which was spoken by God must in the very nature of things be all embracing, perfect,

---

1. *Zevachim* 115b: "Said R. Ishmael, the general rules were said at Sinai and the details at the Tent of Meeting. R. Akiba said, the general rules and the details were said at Sinai, they were repeated in the Tent of Meeting, and stated a third time in the plains of Moab." See also *Exodus Rabbah,* chap. 32, and passages quoted here in chap. 1 n. 60, Kuzari, Maamar Aleph, para. 87.

and complete. That which God spoke requires but to be
understood, it does not require addition.[2] The Jewish people were fortunate in that God himself showed them,
through the agency of Moses, how to understand, amplify,
and apply His spoken word—both as far as we have it in the
Written Word itself and as it has been handed down,
studied, and applied by tradition, the Oral Law. The conclusion to be drawn from this is that the entire Torah, in the
broadest sense of the term, embracing Bible, Oral Law,
tradition, and the organic development based upon these,
is to be discovered in the Decalogue.[3]

The Rabbis comment on the verse,[4] "And on them
(the two tablets) was written according to all the words God
spoke with you in the mount," as follows:[5]

It goes to teach that God showed Moses in advance all
the subtle details of the biblical law and its scribal
interpretation.

On the same verse the Midrash Kohelet[6] comments:

2. See *Bamidbar Rabbah,* chap. 13. Annaf Yoseph n. 15. According to the opinion in Shir Rabbah, chap. 1, only the first two statements
of the Decalogue were said by God to the people. TaRYaG is embraced
by these two alone.

3. It is this concept that underlay the controversy with the Minim,
who declared that only the Decalogue is divine law, and led to the
abandonment of the public recitation of the Decalogue. *Berakhot* 12a
and Rashi ad loc. Jerusalem *Berakhot,* chap. 1, *Challah* 5. See also
Zevin HaMoadim BeHalachah (Tel Aviv, 1949), pp. 324–325, and M. J.
Gvariahu, *Sinai* 22: 5–6: 367 et seq.

4. Deuteronomy 9:10.

5. *Megillah* 196.

6. Chap. 1.

The words, the Rabbis state, embody Holy Writ, Mishnah, Toseftot, Haggadot, and all that a conscientious student may develop from them in the future.

A further relevant passage is quoted by Ginzberg[7] and reads:

Between the separate commandments (of the Decalogue) were noted down all the precepts of the Torah in all their particulars.

With this general background in mind, the tradition of grouping the laws of the Torah under the generalized headings of the Decalogue is seen to be an integral aspect of the traditional view of Torah as a whole. The earliest known attempt to classify and treat the mitzvot under the general headings of the Decalogue is found, as has been stated, in the writings of Philo,[8] while in the Middle Ages this manner of treatment became fairly general.[9]

The grouping of the mitzvot under the headings of the Decalogue naturally led to Torah, TaRYaG, and the two tablets of stone being regarded as synonymous.[10] TaRYaG

---

7. *Legends*, vol. 3, p. 119. Cf. Jerusalem *Shekalim*, chap. 6; Shir. Rabbah sec. 5.

8. See here chap. 3 n. 32.

9. Cf., e.g., Abarbanel to Exodus, chap. 20; Ibn Ezra and Gersonides on the Decalogue. Few authorities agree on the exact division of the mitzvot within this framework. For an independent grouping see Otzar Yisrael, erech Asseret Ḥadibrot. Also "TaRYaG Precepts," in *The Works of Nachmanides*, ed. Chavell, vol. 2 (Jerusalem, 1964), pp. 521–548.

10. For TaRYaG equated with two tablets, See Jerusalem *Shekalim*, chap. 6, *Challah* 1. Jerusalem *Sotah*, chap. 8, *Challah* 3. Jerusalem *Taanit*, chap. 4, *Challah* 5. Babylonian *Shabbat* 87a and related pas-

becomes inseparable from the Decalogue, which embraces that number of precepts.[11] The statement in *Bamidbar Rabbah*[12] that

> The tablets contain TaRYaG mitzvot represented by
> the letters "*I am*" to "*unto Thy neighbor,*" neither less
> nor more[13]

simply reflects this in a categorical manner.

The equation of TaRYaG with the Decalogue gave
rise[14] to one form of the type of literature called Azharot,[15]

---

sages. Cf. also Abot D'Rabbi Nathan, chap. 2, where appears the
statement: "He (Moses) said, how can I give Israel these tablets? I am
forcing upon them stringent commandments that carry the death
penalty, for it is written (Exodus 22:19), "He who sacrifices to any god,
save unto the Lord alone, shall be utterly destroyed." See also note of
Binyan Yehoshua, ad loc. The identification of TaRYaG with Torah led
to several observations on the part of various scholars. On the sefer
Torah, which the king is obligated to have with him at all times (see
Deuteronomy 17), the Baalei Hatosaphot explained, "There was written in it only the Decalogue, but since from "I am" to "unto thy
neighbor" there are 613 letters, which represent the TaRYaG mitzvot, it
is called a Sefer Torah." Ibn Ezra quotes Saadyah Gaon to similar effect
in his commentary to Deuteronomy 27:1, as does Kimchi on Joshua
8:32. The statement in the Talmud, *Berakhot* 18a, to the effect that "a
person should not enter a cemetery with Tefillin on his head and a
Sefer Torah on his arm," was understood by R. Nachshon Gaon (quoted
in Arukh, erekh, Tefillah, Tevel) to refer to the Decalogue, which
contains TaRYaG letters for the TaRYaG mitzvot.

11. See Rashi and Targum Jonathan on Exodus 24:12.

12. Chap. 18.

13. It is possible that in the addition of the words "neither less nor
more," we have the faded echoes of an ancient controversy concerning the actual number of biblical precepts. However, the reading of this
passage in the Tanchuma, Kora. omits these words.

14. Cf. the introductory words of Ibn Gabirol to his famous
Azharah, Shemor Libbi Maaneh: "At Sinai were they appointed, from

namely Piyyut,[16] which takes each statement of the Decalogue to refer to a group of mitzvot, or each letter of the
Decalogue to represent a particular mitzvah, and lists the
mitzvot accordingly. The origin of the Azharah is partially
bound up with the general development of the Piyyut,
more especially with the halachic Piyyut. In fact several
halachic Piyyutim, although having no connection with
the TaRYaG Azharot, are called Azharot.[17]

The Piyyut itself is at least as old as the Tannaitic
period, the third-century contemporary of R. Judah the
Prince, R. Eliezer b. R. Shimon, being the earliest recorded
Payytan,[18] while piyyutistic activity was not lacking during the period of the Amoraim[19] However, the first great
flowering of the Piyyut is generally admitted to have been
in the period after the closing of the Talmud, when the

---

on high were they heard, they were together embedded in the ten
words."

15. The meanings of the word Azharah are:

a) A warning given in the case of a biblical prohibition, Ben
Yehudah, *Dictionary*, vol. 1, p. 124.

b) Throughout the midrashim "warning" is also used in connection with positive precepts (Leviticus Rabbah 30:3, etc.).

c) A term expressing punishment. Guttman, Clavis Talmudis
(Budapest, 1917), vol. 2, p. 180. Elbogen in *Encyclopedia Eshkol*,
heading Azharah, suggests that the term Azharah came to be
used for this type of Piyyut because the numerical equivalent of
Azharat is TaRYaG, *Alef*=1. *Zayyin*=7. *Heh*=5. *Resh*=200.
Taw=400, and it is therefore an appropriate title for a poem whose
purpose is to list TaRYaG mitzvot.

16. Piyyut, Paitanim, from Gr. Poietria and Poietes, Waxman, *History of Jewish Literature*, 2nd ed., vol. 1, p. 205.

17. Elbogen. An outstanding example is that found in the morning
service for the Sabbath preceding Passover. See Otzar HaTefillot
(Vilna, 1914), pt. 2, p. 241.

18. Leviticus Rabbah, chap. 30.

19. Luzzatto, Introduction to the Machzor Italiani (Livorno, 1860),
p. 7.

daily prayers had received more or less fixed form,[20] to achieve unsurpassed productivity in the work of Yose ben Yose and Yannai, both of whom probably flourished in seventh-century Palestine.

Originally the Piyyut was arranged to be recited after, and separate from, the actual order of prayer.[21] Indeed, the Geonim fought long and hard against piyyutistic additions to the liturgy,[22] and only because people used to leave the synagogue at the conclusion of the regular service were the piyyutim brought into the actual service itself.[23] This is true of Piyyutim such as the Avodah of Yom Kippur as well as for the Azharot of Shavuot. The actual recitation of these latter during the Pentecost Service was disapproved of by so late a scholar as Avudraham, who says,[24]

> And others recite them (the Azharot) *after* the repetition of the (Mussaf) Tefillah, in order to avoid interrupting the Tefillah itself, and this is correct.

And the Machzor Italiani, although confirming the custom to recite the Azharot during the reader's repetition of the Mussaf, nevertheless records[25] that "in order to make no interruption in the Tefillah, our custom in Venice is to recite them before Ashrei." However, the inclusion in the Siddur of Rab Amram Gaon[26] of the Azharot in the middle of the

20. Ibid.

21. Ibid.

22. Ginzberg, *Geonica,* vol. 1, p. 122. See also J. H. Zimmels, *Ashkenazim and Sefardim* (London, 1958), p. 101, and notes ad. loc. on the involved problem of recital of Piyyut during prayer.

23. Luzzatto, p. 7.

24. *Sefer Avudraham* (Warsaw, 1877), p. 121.

25. Machzor Italiani, pp. 154 and 157.

26. (Warsaw, 1865), p. 43.

Mussaf prayer shows that as the general opposition to the inclusion of the Piyyut had failed, so had it failed to prevent the incursion of the Azharot into the Mussaf prayer.

The inclusion of the TaRYaG Azharot in the order of service forms part of the general characteristics of including halachic material in the liturgy.[27] but in addition to forming part of this general characteristic, their inclusion, which does not offer the reader any practical halachic guidance, since the TaRYaG Azharah is simply a factual enumeration of TaRYaG and nothing more,[28] is due to other factors.

During the festival of Shavuot, traditionally the "Season of the Giving of the Law," the Torah reading in the synagogue for the first day of the festival consists of the Ten Commandments. The danger of heresy[29] was in itself sufficient reason for he amplification of the Decalogue on this occasion, when it forms the center of the service. The recitation of the Ten Commandments as part of the regular service[30] had been forcibly abandoned in talmudic times. Did not this public recitation constitute a possible danger? Indeed, it was owing to this possible danger that Maimonides in a celebrated responsum[31] chided those who ascribed special significance to the Decalogue by standing when it was read, and forbade it. The actual

---

27. Ismar Elbogen, Judische Gottesdienst in Seiner Geschichtlichen Entwicklung (Leipzig, 1913), p. 217.

28. Of course in its later form it achieved a poetic beauty of its own, although even in the hands of Ibn Gabirol the Azharah lost none of its obscurity as far as the actual TaRYaG list is concerned.

29. See this chapter n. 3.

30. Mishnah *Tamid* 5:1. See also W. O. E. Oesterly and T. H. Robinson, an introduction to the Books of the Old Testament (Meridian Books, 1958), p. 14 n. 2.

31. Moses ben Maimon, *Responsa,* ed. A. Frieman (Jerusalem, 1934), no. 46.

custom of reading the Decalogue on Shavuot is at variance with the Mishnah[32] and is dependent for its validity on the Tosefta[33] which is the finally accepted view expressed in the Talmud.[34]

Thus, according to rabbinic opinion, the Azharot filled a substantial need. There remained no loophole for a declaration to the effect that only the Decalogue is the word of God, since the reading of the Decalogue was immediately followed by one or other of the Azharot, which detailed the 613 mitzvot of the Torah.[35]

The actual origin of the Azharah is probably to be found in the inherent popularity of the TaRYaG tradition, and, in addition to the reason already outlined, this popularity must have played a decisive role in bringing the Azharah into the synagogue service. The very fact that in spite of their early appearance the Azharot never assumed any definite form tends to confirm the view that their prime function was not that of the ordinary Piyyut, but rather to fill a popular need for the reduction of a generally held principle to factual terms,[36] even if only in a very general manner.

Before proceeding to the problem of dating the Azharot, it is necessary to examine carefully the work of the Ba'al Halachot Gedolot in this connection.[37]

---

32. *Megillah* 3:5.

33. *Megillah 3:3. Cf. also tractate Soferim,* chap. 17, Hal. 6.

34. *Megillah* 31a.

35. It is, however, of interest to note that in some rites the Azharot were not recited on Shavuot at all. For example, the Azharah of Elijah the Danite appears in the Machzor Minhag Hodu (Amsterdam, 1688), for recital on Shemini Atzeret, probably in preparation for Simchat Torah, when the reading of the entire Torah is concluded.

36. Guttman, p. 13.

37. Further problems in connection with this work will be discussed in chap. 5.

It has been assumed[38] on the basis of Maimonides' statement in the preface to his *Sefer HaMitzvot,*

> similarly the numerous Azharot, written in the land of Spain, which I have heard, have caused me distress because I see them as popularizing the matter. And although the authors are not to be blamed, for they are poets and not scholars,[39] and that which is fitting to their work they have accomplished in pleasant style and beautiful arrangement, nevertheless, in the understanding of the matter they have followed the Ba'al Halachot Gedolot and other later Rabbis,[40]

that the Azharot postdate the *Halachot Gedolot.* However, apart from blaming the author of the *Halachoth* for the mistakes of the Azharot current in his time, all that may legitimately be inferred from Maimonides' words is that the Azharot found "in Spain" postdate the *Halachot Gedolot,* and in his (Maimonides') opinion their errors are due to unreasonable fidelity to BeHaG's opinions.

Maimonides reproves not only the authors of the Azharot but also certain Rabbanim,[41] because "as fools

---

38. Eisenstein, *Otzar Yisrael,* vol. 1, p. 226. M. Slutzky, preface to the Azharah of Elijah Hazaken (Warsaw, 1900), p. ix n. 12.

39. The reference is directed against Ibn Gabirol; see Heller, ad. loc n. 34.

40. This and the following two quotations from the preface of the S.H. are taken from my own unpublished translation of the S.H.

41. These are identified Heller, ad. loc. n. 29, as R. Nissim and Chefetz b. Yazliach. See also Sede Chemed, Klallei Haposkim, Maimonides, no. 21. Maimonides himself (Responsa, Freiman, 240) was not, in his early years, entirely free from such fidelity to authorities such as Chefez. Thus, in answer to a query concerning his interpretation of a mishnah, he writes: "In our explanation we followed the writings of

they have stood (blindly) by the words of the man," and
with bitterly ironical invective he says, "for the mark of the
intelligent in our time does not lie in their examination of a
subject on its own merits, but in (testing) its conformity to
that which has preceded it, without (ever) having (critically) examined the earlier presentation."

Of other Azharot, Maimonides makes no mention, a
point eagerly seized upon by Slutzky himself[42] in order to
explain away, quite legitimately, the scathing terms in
which the Azharot are described, when faced with the
Azharah of Elijah Hazaken, who was one of the most
renowned talmudists of is day.[43]

In any event it is not possible to countenance the post
Halachot Gedolot origin of the Azharot, for the following
cogent reasons:

First, a responsum by R. Natronai Gaon (850–860), the
predecessor of BeHaG,[44] deals with the laxity evinced by
some communities in the recitation of the Azharot.

Second, the automatic acceptance of the recital of
Azharot even in the middle of the Mussaf Tefillah, on the
part of R. Amram Gaon,[45] argues strongly for the antiquity
of the Azharot, since some time must certainly have elap-
sed between the emergence of the Azharah and its acceptance into the actual prayer itself.[46]

---

the S.H. of Chefez, of Blessed Memory. He was mistaken, and in our
having followed his interpretations we failed to fully examine the
subject matter."

42. Ibid., p. viii n. 9.
43. Ibid., p. iii n. 1.
44. Quoted by Guttman, p. 9, from Harkavy, and found in Halachot
Pessukot p. 104.
45. Siddur, p. 43.
46. See chap. 4.

Third, it is hardly possible to ascribe blind adherence to an institution of the author of the *Halachot Gedolot* either by R. Amram Gaon or by the strong-minded Saadya Gaon, who composed not one but two Azharot. Had the custom of reciting Azharot not been firmly rooted and generally widespread, he, in compiling his Siddur for the congregations of his native Egypt,[47] would hardly have undertaken the laboriously involved task of writing Azharot. Saadya himself writes[48] that it is only due to the failings in his eyes[49] of the customary Azharah, "Atta Hinchalta" that "I see fit to replace it with something else," but there is no inkling of any doubt in Saadya's mind as to the propriety of reciting Azharot. On the contrary. Saadya's opinion, quoted by Ibn Ezra,[50] to the effect that the law engraved upon the stones[51] was in reality only TaRYaG in the form of an Azharah, confirms the fact that to Saadya the Azharot were of remote origin.

Finally, the opinions to be adduced below concerning the dates of the composition of the early Azharot completely dispel the notion that the Azharot are a product of the period succeeding BeHaG.

Careful examination of the TaRYaG list that appears at the beginning of the *Halachot Gedolot* brings to light a fact,

---

47. Ginzberg, *Geonica,* vol. 1, p. 167 n. 1.

48. Siddur, p. 156, ed. I. Davidson, S. Assaf and B. L. Joel (Jerusalem, 1941).

49. And yet Maimonides speaks of "blind adherence." Apparently he did not know of Saadya's Azharot. It is difficult, however, to assume ignorance of Saadya's Siddur on the part of Maimonides, who was so long resident in Egypt. Perle, in his lengthy preface to Saadya's enumeration, shows the complete divergence that in fact exists between Saadya's work and that of his predecessor.

50. Commentary to Deuteronomy 27:1.

51. Deuteronomy, chap. 27.

relevant to our discussion, that has been completely overlooked by all who have written on both the Azharot and
the *Halachot Gedolot*.

In the first instance, although in the printed editions
the enumeration of TaRYaG is called a preface, it bears no
resemblance whatsoever to that which we normally understand by the term preface. We are treated to no introduction to the contents of the work that follows, and indeed, no
mention of the book itself is made at all. This section is in
fact completely unattached to the work as a whole and is
enclosed by its own introductory and concluding paragraphs. These consist of quotations from the Talmud and
the Midrash. The introductory paragraph closes with R.
Simlai's statement concerning TaRYaG, adding

> all who observe them merit the life of the world to
> come, while all who transgress them are punished by
> seven types of punishment.

The seven types are then enumerated and the relevant
prohibitions listed under each of the seven headings, the
largest group consisting of 277 prohibitions, transgressions
that involve corporal punishment.

The important point that emerges from this is the
careful, logical classification of the prohibitions. But, in
addition to this sevenfold classification, the large group of
prohibitions involving corporal punishment is also carefully arranged, not in a logical order of the author's own
choosing but, with slight deviation, following the order in
which the prohibitions appear in the Torah. The difference
is only that where the particular prohibitions pertaining to
a given subject are scattered in the Torah, they are for the

most part enumerated together when the subject first appears in the Torah.[52]

In complete contrast to this, the section listing the positive commandments, which follows, lacks any form of coherency or system. Precepts that have absolutely no connection with one another are jumbled together in profusion.[53]

The contrasting manner in which the two groups are put together is patently obvious. Indeed it is surprising that Professor Guttman, in spite of his painstaking analysis of the *Halachot Gedolot*, failed to notice it. However, it is possible to understand what has happened if we bear in mind the fact that the Ba'al *Halachot Gedolot* is not the originator of the TaRYaG lists but was preceded by the Azharot, which were already widespread in his time.

Had he indeed been the originator of the lists, it is difficult to see how he could have simply plunged into the actual list without so much as a hint of the difficulties that have baffled all of his successors. Even if he wished to avoid discussion of the complex problems involved, he should hardly have listed the positive commandments in a manner so terse as to obscure the identity of the individual mitzvot.[54] Contrasted with the order that reigns in the list

---

52. On mentioning the prohibition against Sabbath work, the author continues with the similar prohibitions concerning the festivals and High Holy Days. Reverting to the order in the Torah, "Thou shalt not desire" (Deuteronomy 5:18) follows "Thou shalt not covet" (Exodus 20:14). Linked with Exodus 22:24 is Leviticus 25:37, etc.

53. "Removal of leaven, covering the blood, ritual immersion, vows," all of which appear in one phrase. There are several related small groups of mitzvot scattered here and there, but nothing like a coherent order of enumeration.

54. "To study, to teach, to observe, and to do" are considered by Zohar Hark, p. 30, sec. 17, and by Traub (Warsaw, 1874), p. 10, as four

of prohibitions, this obscurity can hardly be intentional. It is therefore probable that the author of the *Halachot Gedolot*, being dissatisfied with a current list of the prohibitions, compiled his own logically ordered list along the lines outlined above, traces of which ordering are found in the Mishnah itself.[55] Then, in order to complete the enumeration of the precepts, he simply copied out the positive commandments of a current Azharah that conformed to his theories of TaRYaG, without troubling himself as to its terseness or obscurity. This contention receives support from the piyyutistic ending appended to the list in Hildersheimer's edition of the *Halachot Gedolot*[56] and is conclusively illustrated by the fact that the concluding section, called Parashyot,[57] follows the order in which the Parashyot appear in the Torah without deviation. Bounded thus on both sides by the order of precepts in the Torah, the middle section is certainly anomalous.

From all that has been said it appears that far from the Azharot having sprung from the *Halachot Gedolot*, the reverse seems to have been the case, the author of the *Halachot* having used a current Azharah for his own purpose.

Understood thus, the silence of the Ba'al *Halachot Gedolot* on the complicated problems involved in listing TaRYaG is understandable; he was simply affording status to a prevalent custom, he was not inventing it.[58]

---

mitzvot, in addition to which the mitzvah "to study Torah" appears separately. Similarly, "to cleave unto God, to walk in His ways, to clothe the naked, to bury the dead, to visit the sick" are considered by Maimonides, Root One, as five mitzvot, whereas Nachmanides holds that only one mitzvah is intended. Examples could be multiplied.

55. See the detailed analysis by Guttman, p. 16 et seq.

56. Quoted by Guttman, p. 10, and there discussed by him at length.

57. On the Parashyot, see here chap. 5.

58. If indeed, as it would seem, the list of positive commandments

II

On the basis of the characteristics of the pre-Islamic period of influence upon Hebrew poetry, Luzzatto[59] concludes that the Azharah "Atta Hinchalta" certainly antedates the *Halachot Gedolot*. The ascription of this Azharah to Elijah Hazaken has no basis in fact,[60] while Rappaport's opinion[61] to the effect that R. Shimeon of Mens(?) is the author is equally groundless.[62] The fact remains that the authorship of this Azharah, like that of the equally famous Azharat Reshit, is unknown,[63] although Zunz[64] is of the opinion that the origin of Azharat Reshit is to be found in Pumpedita.

Of the two, Azharat Reshit is the older,[65] and it has indeed been suggested[66] that the very title Azharah owes itself to the opening words of this Piyyut. The simple style of early Azharot places them in the period of the Saboraim.[67]

---

is simply a borrowed Azharah, it would substantiate the fact that even among the early Azharot, some at least enjoyed a logical division of sorts, even though this might only have been confined to division into the broad fields of positive and prohibitive commandments.

59. Preface to Machzor Italiani, pp. 8, 10, and 26.

60. Ibid., p. 26. In any event, as we have already seen in chap. 4, the Azharah Atta Hinchaltah is quoted by Saadya.

61. Cf. also Dr. M. Sacks, ed., *Festgebete der Israeliten* (Breslau, 1907), pt. 9, p. 194. This opinion is based upon the responsum of Marshall, quoted by Heidenheim in the Rodelheim Machzor (1857), Shavuoth, p. 72.

62. Landshuth, *Amudei Ha'avodah* (Berlin, 1856), pt. 2, p. 312.

63. Zunz, *Literatur Geschichte der Synagogalen Poesie* (Berlin, 1865), pp. 4 and 21.

64. Ibid., p. 21 and n. 2; see below on this point.

65. I. Elbogen, Judische Gottesidienst, p. 218, not as Halper, *Jewish Quarterly Review* April 1914, 524.

66. Elbogen, *Encyclopedia*, vol. 2, p. 32.

67. Dr. M. Sacks, quoted by Slutzky, preface to Azharah of Elijah Hazaken, p. ix. In the case of Azharat Reshit, the internal evidence

It has been pointed out[68] on the basis of several extant manuscripts[69] that in spite of the anonymity that surrounds these two Azharot, both enjoy superscriptions that point to their remote and Babylonian origin. At the end of Azharat Reshit are found the words,

Azharot of the Rabbis,

and in a second manuscript,

Azharot of the Holy College of the Rabbis of Pumpedita,

while at the end of Atta Hinchaltah are found,

Azharot of Elijah the Tishbite,[70] may his memory be for a blessing,

and

---

might well suggest that it belongs to the period before the Saboraim and is to be attributed to the late Amoraim. In enumerating the various branches of Torah received at Sinai, the Azharah says, "Examined Halachot and Orders Six, and in addition Talmud Thirty-Six." Now in fact there are thirty-seven tractates in the Talmud, but the thirty-seventh, *Tamid*, was only arranged during the Saboraic period (see *Otzar Yisrael*, headings Talmud and *Tamid*. But see A. Weiss, *The Babylonian Talmud as a literary unit (New York, 1943), p. 53 and n. 106). It is therefore understandable that if the author of the Azharah lived before the Saboraim, he knew of only thirty-six tractates.*

68. Luzzatto, p. 24; Zunz, p. 23; Elbogen, p. 558; Landshuth, p. 313.

69. The missing reference in Landshuth for Azharat Reshit is found in Zunz, p. 21 n. 2. It is codex Hamburg, h. 240.

70. The Machzor Bologna (1541), has the ending "Azharat of Elijah, may his memory be for a blessing." This is doubtless the origin as pointed out by Dukes (Literaturblatt, 1849), no. 26, p. 406, of the mistaken ascription of these Azharot to Elijah Hazaken.

Azharot of Elijah the prophet,

and

Azharot of the Rabbis of the College.

It has already been mentioned that Saadya Gaon found the custom of reciting Atta Hinchaltah entrenched in his time,[71] and it is more than likely that the Azharot mentioned by R. Amram Gaon[72] are the same ones. Having been included by R. Amram when he sent his order of Prayers to Spain,[73] they later spread throughout Europe and have since remained inseparable from the Ashkenazi Machzor. Since both of these Geonim were of Sura, it may be assumed that the prevalent custom in Sura was to read Atta Hinchaltah. Azharat Reshit, on the other hand, bears a superscription identifying it with the College of Pumpedita. It is therefore probable that the two colleges differed in the recitation of the Piyyutim, as they differed in so many customs. A comparison of the two Azharot readily suggests the reason for this divergence.

Atta Hinchaltah is an extremely long Piyyut involving a fully detailed enumeration of the mitzvot. It was originally divided into ten sections[74] and the mitzvot are listed according to various acrostical arrangements of the Hebrew alphabet. Azharat Reshit, on the other hand, contains no arrangement of the mitzvot at all. After stating,

---

71. Siddur, p. 156.

72. p. 43. But see Jellineck, Kontres TaRYaG, Ma'arecheth Hasephorim no. 5.

73. Ginzberg, *Geonica*, vol. 1, p. 121.

74. On the fact that several mitzvot are missing from the Azharah as we have it, see Luzzatto, p. 26; ad Landshuth, p. 313, bottom.

Thou hast given to Thy people positive commandments and prohibitions; in number 365 as the number
of days in the solar year; and 248 positive commandments as the number of limbs in the human body,

it proceeds to list all the branches of Torah and tradition as
being of divine origin.

Slutzky[75] is of the opinion that Azharat Reshit "also
included an enumeration of TaRYaG but was shortened by
the printers, who left only the introduction and conclusion." But this is not so, since all the early manuscripts of
this Azharah have it in exactly the same form as it appears
in the printed editions. Indeed, Menachem b. Joseph, the
Reader at Troyes (twelfth century), says,[76]

It is good to recite the Azharah "Emeth Yehegeh
Chikki," on the first day, in honor of Elijah Hazaken
(its author), and all the mitzvot are well listed therein
in a pleasant manner. However, Azharat Reshit is
older, and I have heard that in it *are hinted*[77] all the
commandments; and some recite it on the first day
and Emet Yehege on the second day, because of the
fear of wearying the congregation, who have partici-
pated at length in the reading of the Ten Commandments on the first day,

from which it is obvious that Azharat Reshit did not contain a lengthy enumeration of the precepts and was therefore preferred for the first day's service, which was in any
event unduly lengthened by the recital of Akkdamot.

---

75. Preface, p. ix n. 12.
76. Mahzor Troyes (Frankfurt Main, 1905), p. 34.
77. My italics.

The importance of this Azharah lies in its stress upon the fact that all the details and ramifications of Torah were received at Sinai, and for that reason it was found appropriate for recital on the day the revelation was read in the synagogue.[78]

With this difference in the nature of the two Azharot in mind, the divergent custom of the academies would seem to lie in a basic difference of approach toward the subject of TaRYaG as a whole. Both unquestionably concurred in the TaRYaG tradition, but they were at variance in connection with the problems involved in its detailed enumeration. The Sura Academy apparently felt the need for such a detailed list,[79] while the Pumpeditans considered the difficulties in producing a definitive list too great to be overcome, and they therefore contented themselves with the mere reiteration of the tradition, as stated in Azharat Reshit, with no amplification whatsoever.

In this regard, it is not without significance that Saadya Gaon of Sura wrote two enumerations of the mitzvot, for it was he who engaged in polemic against the Karaites.[80] He must surely have been aware of the "lists of laws" in which the Karaites attempted to enumerate the biblical precepts after their own fashion. He, above all others, must have felt most keenly the need, upheld by his academy, for a detailed list of TaRYaG, if only to counter this growing menace to traditional Judaism.

---

78. See here, chap. 4.

79. According to a Epstein, L. Ginsberg, and others, R. Shimon Kayyira compiled the *Halachot Gedolot* in Sura, circa 825. See Tzernowitz, Told. Hap., vol. 1, p. 70 n. 25.

80. On Saadya's polemic against the Karaites, see, *Jewish Quarterly Review,* new series 3 (1917–1918): 166 et seq., and Malter, pp. 280ff. pp. 380–394, for his polemic in general. Saadya's work on TaRYaG was written in Sura, between 922–928; see Malter, p. 150.

The difference in custom on the part of the academies in connection with the Azharot might also have a more subtle reason. The long struggle waged by the Geonim against the Piyyut had finally failed, or at best had ended in a compromise.[81] Ginzberg[82] states that,

"in general, the investigator gains the impression that the Geonim of Sura were by far more kindly disposed toward the Piyyut than those of Pumpedita.

This being so, the divergent custom surrounding the Azharot is easily explained. The Pumpeditans, who were opposed in principle to the Piyyut but who were forced in the course of time to acquiesce in its inclusion in the service, preferred to keep the Piyyut to a minimum, whereas the Sura Academy, being more kindly disposed toward the Piyyut, included the long Azharah in its order of service.

III

In examining the strictures of Maimonides upon the authors of the Azharot, it is important to bear in mind both the difficulties inherent in enumerating TaRYaG, and the purpose that these writers had in mind. In spite of the fact that Saadya Gaon, by including the reading of the *Megillah* and the kindling of Chanukkah lights in his enumeration,[83] lays himself open to Maimonides' strictures in Root

---

81. *Geonica*, vol. 1, p. 122 n. 1.
82. Ibid.
83. Siddur, p. 157. Also *Sefer HaMitzvot* of R. Saadya Gaon, ed. S. Halpern (Jerusalem, 1930), p. 2.

One,[84] he can hardly be upbraided as being either un-learned or a blind follower of the author of the *Halachot Gedolot*. Maimonides himself experienced the greatest difficulty in compiling his TaRYaG list,[85] and the difficulties experienced by virtually every other scholar, including Aaron of Barcelona, who follows Maimonides even when he realizes that right is with critic,[86] tend to show that even a thoroughly logical approach to the problem is not with-out its drawbacks. BeHaG, Chefetz b. Yatzliach,[87] and others used different systems in working out their enumer-ations; and while Maimonides certainly applied tremen-dous acumen in his fundamentalist approach, the doubtful cases that nevertheless remain support Nachmanides' con-tention that "Elijah will solve this matter.[88]

This being so, we may readily understand the inac-curacies of the authors of Azharot, especially in view of the fact that their aim was more to provide a summary of the content of Torah than a halachically sound[89] exposition of TaRYaG. They were intent upon teaching a general lesson to the public in accessible form; they were not

---

84. Halpern's attempted vindication of Saadya, preface, is not con-vincing. As far as *Megillah* is concerned, I do not feel that Saadya is open to criticism at all. His words are "Ketov Zoth Remez Limeg-gillah," which simply means that Saadya considered the words "Ketov Zoth" (Exodus 17:14) to be a positive commandment, later fulfilled by the compilation of the Book of Esther.

85. See chap. 1 of this study.

86. Chinuch, mitzvah 573.

87. See chap. 5.

88. See chap. 1 of this study.

89. Of course this does not mean that their exposition of TaRYaG is not halachically sound from the point of view of their own understand-ing of the Halachah involved. Tosafot quotes Azharot as halachic authority in several instances, e.g., *Sukkah* 49a, *Yoma* 8a, Babylonian *Batah* 145b, etc.; also Or Zarua, Hilchot Keriat Shema, siman 19.

writing for halachic experts. There was no reason for them to shrink from the inclusion of established rabbinic ordinances[90] or even moral aphorisms contained in the Bible.[91] They were certainly well aware of the problem presented by their subject matter, and even Ibn Gabirol, against whom Maimonides' remarks are directed in particular, and who we are somewhat scornfully informed "was a poet and not a Rabbi," states at the commencement of "Shemor Libbi Maneh," the most famous and widespread of all the Azharot,

> And He will forgive the guilt, And He will increase the strength, And He will bestow the wisdom to make mortals understand,

which beautiful passage is rightly understood by Duran[92] and R. Menachem of Troyes[93] to reflect the poet's heart-searchings in attempting to enumerate the precepts of God. He fully appreciates his own shortcomings as well as the difficulties involved, and one feels the dread that makes him hesitant when he says, "and He who reveals things hidden will cover up my sin." Despite the fact that Gabirol relies upon the enumeration of the *Halachot Gedolot*, he cannot free himself from the thought that if some error had indeed crept into the former work, he, Gabirol, would be guilty before God of perpetuating and popularizing it.

---

90. Possibly in view of the ancient tradition that the Ketter Torah, the 620 letters in the Decalogue, embraced TaRYaG and the seven rabbinic laws.

91. E.g., Leviticus 25:36, included both by BeHaG and Saadya. But see Zohar Harakia, p. 41, sec. 39.

92. Ibid., p. 25, sec. 2.

93. Machzor Bologna, commentary to this Azharah.

IV

Saadya Gaon's Azharot, which succeeded in entering no liturgy, certainly contain a radically new approach to the whole subject. In grouping TaRYaG under the ten headings of the Decalogue,[94] the enumeration ceases to be haphazard as in the early Azharah. The grouping together of the mitzvot involves close examination of their inner relationship to one another, as well as to the particular statement of the Decalogue to which they are attached. This method of arranging TaRYaG was widely followed, even the exact number of precepts assigned to each group by Saadya appearing in the Ma'amar Hasskel,[95] although the Ma'amar differs in the actual detailed enumeration of the precepts.

Other famous Azharot, such as Elijah Hazaken's "Emeth Yehege Chikki"[96] and R. Isaac Algerbeloni's "Ayzeh Mekkom Binah,"[97] follow independent arrangements.[98] Throughout the

---

94. According to Saadya there are eighty precepts under the first heading, sixty under the second, forty-eight under the third, seventy-eight under the fourth, seventy-seven under the fifth, fifty under the sixth, eighty-eight under the seventh, ninety-nine under the eighth, fifty-two under the ninth, and fifty-four under the tenth.

95. This Ma'amar is wrongly ascribed by Heidenheim (Rodelheim, 1804) to R. Eliezer b. Nathan. The Cremona, ed. 1577, has the name of the author in acrostical form; it was one Samuel b. Yehudah.

96. First published by Luzzatto in Orient, 1850, edition with introduction and explanatory notes by W. Slutzky (Warsaw, 1900).

97. In Minchat Bikkurim (Livorno, 1837). The editor's name does not appear on the frontispiece. But see Jellineck, Kontres TaRYaG, no. 88, who says that the commentaries are by Isaac b. Amzog.

98. There are several literary curiosities in this field, e.g., the attempt by Elijah Ettinger to show that TaRYaG are contained in the four verses of Moses' prayer, Deuteronomy 3:23–26, and Shirah Lechayyim (Warsaw, 1817), which attempts to insert TaRYaG into the 613 letters of Shirath Ha'azinu.

ages, numerous Azharot[99] and poems[100] have been compiled with TaRYaG as their theme. One's amazement is
invoked on contemplating those poems, which successfully tackle the task of taking each letter of the Decalogue to represent a member of TaRYaG and then construct
a 613-line poem, each line containing one mitzvah and
each line commencing with the letters of the Decalogue as
they appear in the text. The outstanding example of this
form, in clear, easy-flowing, rhyming couplets, is that of R.
David Vittal's Ketter Torah.[101]

99. See Ben Yaacob, *Otzar Seforim*, p. 361 et seq. Kontress TaRYaG
Maarechet Haseforim. Mention might be made of two Azharot that
follow Maimonides' enumeration, the one by Isaac Kimchi of
Provence, the other by Joshua Benveniste.

100. Ibid. and *Otzar Yisrael*, vol. 1, p. 226.

101. Third edition (Jerusalem, 1882). Vittal follows Maimonides in
the enumeration of the precepts. Vittal appends an original classification of the precepts, dividing them into eighteen groups.

5

The Geonic Period

In spite of the early currency of the TaRYaG tradition, it is only during the latter part of the Geonic period that the tradition comes to be treated with the care and attention it deserves. It is during the late Geonic period that TaRYaG assumes definite form and objective as well as relationship to Torah in the wider sense.

In surveying the period to the time of Maimonides, it is noticeable that no two authors treat the tradition in exactly the same manner. In view of this diversity, one is perhaps justified in asking whether—and if so, to what extent—a general attitude toward TaRYaG characterizes the authors of this period?

The major TaRYaG works of the period may be classified as follows:

	Form	Treatment	Object
1. Sheiltot	midrashic code	popular	halachic
2. *Halachot Gedolot*	Azharah	popular	Indeterminate/ indirectly halachic
3. Saadya Gaon	Azharah	popular	Introduction of system with definite theological outlook concerning the Decalogue
4. Saadya Gaon	code	halachic	halachic
5. Chefez b. Yatzliach	code	halachic	halachic/ philosophical/ ethical presentation of Judaism
6. Shmuel b. Chofni	code	halachic	halachic

Of these six major works it will be seen that four have a definite halachic object and one has Halachah as its indirect object, while the treatment of the subject is equally distributed between the popular and the strictly halachic approach.

It would seem, therefore, that the approach of the Geonim to TaRYaG was that of an approach to a halachic study and was occasioned by the inherent and widespread popularity of the tradition. The exceptions to the strictly halachic objective are also conditioned by the popularity of the tradition but use the fact of popularity in order to further particular perceptions. This is especially obvious in the case of Saadya Gaon.

This analysis further substantiates the thesis outlined in chapter 2 as to the halachic nature of TaRYaG and clearly shows that Maimonides himself was merely following an already well defined approach to TaRYaG in considering the tradition as a strict Halachah.

A further fact of historical importance is brought to light by means of this listing. It will be shown below that the halachic/TaRYaG works of both Saadya and Chefetz consisted of codes whose scope embraced the entire corpus of Jewish law, and that both used TaRYaG as their starting point. It would seem therefore that Maimonides, in evolving his *Mishneh Torah* from his *Sefer HaMitzvot*, is again but following lines laid down by his predecessors. The differences between Maimonides and his predecessors are twofold. Whereas Saadya and Chefetz use their introductions for the same purposes to which Maimonides devotes his Fourteen Roots, they do not list out TaRYaG individually, without elaboration, as does Maimonides, who in his *Sefer HaMitzvot* separates the TaRYaG list from its ramifications. Second, while the former authors employ Arabic as their medium of expression throughout, Maimonides employed Arabic for TaRYaG and Hebrew for his code.

Although a further reason for Maimonides' use of Arabic will be suggested below, it is possible that the reason lies in the fact that when he commenced his *Sefer HaMitzvot* and adopted both the approach and form of his predecessors, he adopted also their language. He was later to regret this fact.[1]

TaRYaG as a subject broadens tremendously in the hands of Saadya and Chefetz. Although it is only with Maimonides that the scope of the tradition is finally transformed into the science of Halachah, it is already fact with

---

1. Responsum no. 368.

the earlier authors. The attention paid to Maimonides' work, at the expense of his predecessors, is due on the one hand to the tremendous criticisms leveled at them by Maimonides, and on the other to the fact that the former works were lost to posterity before being translated into Hebrew. Thus Maimonides dominated the TaRYaG field.

Both in Saadya and Chefetz, and explicit transformation has already overtaken the TaRYaG concept. The TaRYaG code of biblical law is organically bound up with the Oral Law, the biblical code being considered as simply unidentifiable without a fundamental approach to the science of Halachah. TaRYaG visibly assumes the position of the cornerstone of Torah as a whole, and it can only be understood by means of the entire content of Torah in its widest sense.

Although in relation to the halachic literature as a whole enumerations of TaRYaG play only a very secondary role, it is worthy to note that the very earliest halachic compilation committed to writing after the close of the Talmud deals with TaRYaG.

I

The earliest[2] halachic author whose name has been preserved is R. Acha of Shabcha (680–752), the author of the Sheiltot discussions. Scholars are at variance as to whether the work was compiled in Palestine[3] or in Bablyon.[4] However this may be, the purpose of the Sheiltot, in contrast with the rest of the Geonic literature that has come down to

---

2. See Ginzberg, *Geonica*, vol. 1, p. 77. Assaph, Tekupat Hageonim Vesiphrutta (Jerusalem, 1955), p. 154.

3. Ginzberg, *Geonica*, p. 75 et seq.

4. Assaph, p. 161.

us, is generally agreed to have been directed toward the needs of those possessed of neither the willpower nor ability to continually immerse themselves in the study of Torah.[5] This circumstance accounts for the wealth of aggadic and sermonic material with which the halachic sections are surrounded, as well as for the fact that the entire work is grouped around the pericopes of the Torah as arranged for weekly reading in the synagogue.

As it stands, the Sheiltot comprises 171 discussions that embrace 68 positive precepts, 77 prohibitions, 29 rabbinic ordinances, and fourteen rabbinic prohibitions. But there is no doubt that much of it is missing.[6] Ibn Daud, in his Sefer Hakabballah,[7] has this to say:

> R. Acha of Shabcha was greatly learned, he compiled discussions on all the mitzvot of the Torah, and the book is in our possession to this day,

from which it is clear that not only has but a portion of the original work come down to us but that its original scope was nothing less than an enumeration of TaRYaG,[8] which seems still to have been extant in the time of RABaD, the author of the Sefer Hakabballah (d. 1180).

The Sheiltot represents no dry, factual listing of the precepts. On the contrary, its freshness and originality of

---

5. Assaph rejects completely the imputation of polemic intention on the part of the Sheiltot. Ginzberg, following his opinion that the work was compiled in Palestine, claims (p. 92), that their prime purpose was to introduce the Babylonian Talmud to the Palestinians.

6. See Epstein, *Jewish Quarterly Review* new series 4: 420–423, where newly discovered Sheiltot are printed.

7. Quoted by Assaph, p. 154.

8. Cf. Waxman. *History of Jewish Literature,* 2nd. ed., vol. 1, p. 283.

approach succeeds in clothing each precept with life and adorning it with meaning. No logical listing of TaRYaG is attempted. Since the aim of the work was "popular," the mitzvot are discussed not in the order of their appearance in the Torah but in the pericope where most can be made of them from a homiletical and moral point of view. In this R. Acha is unique in early Jewish literature. Whereas the enumerators of TaRYaG, with the exception of Saadya Gaon, who finds four, are of the opinion that Genesis contains but three precepts,[9] R. Acha, using the narratives of the book as his base, compiled no less than thirty-seven of the extant 171 discussions on Genesis.

A fact of great importance, which will be discussed more fully below, lies in R. Acha's use of the Written Law as the starting point for halachic discourse, which represents quite a radical turning away from talmudic precedent. The reason for this lies in the popular aim of the work. Whereas acquaintance with the intricacies of the Talmud could not be assumed, the same was not true of the Bible and its narratives, which therefore provided an ideal setting for a homiletical, halachic discourse.

The work that surpassed the Sheiltot, because it set out to be a halachic code, was the *Halachot Gedolot*,[10] which was prefaced by a TaRYaG enumeration. We have already dealt with one aspect of this enumeration,[11] and it is our intention here to offer a solution to the major internal problem of the enumeration, which has baffled those who

---

9. Genesis 1:28 (according to some, the precept is derived from Genesis 9:1), Genesis 17:10, and Genesis 32:33. Saadya considers circumcision to embrace two positive precepts.

10. On the involved problems surrounding the authorship and date of this work, see *Geonica*, vol. 1, p. 99 et seq., and Assaph, p. 168 ff.

11. Chap. 4.

have dealt with it hitherto. Before doing so, however, it seems pertinent to explain why the list appears at all.

It is true that Anan's "book of abominations that he calls the book of precepts"[12] was making itself felt, as was his attempt "to make a Talmud of his own."[13] But although the Karaite activity might well suggest a reason for the *need* for such a list, the absolute lack of any polemic in the *Halachot Gedolot* precludes its being thought of primarily as an anti-Karaite work. Indirectly, as the first halachic code to be committed to writing since the close of the Talmud, its countereffect to Karaism, simply by virtue of its clear statement of the traditional Halachah, must have been considerable.[14] In any event the Karaite menace was probably the prime mover in this final breaking away from the centuries-old tradition that looked askance at the committal of Halachah to writing. Karaism therefore does play some part in the emergence of the work, but the key to the TaRYaG preface lies in the nature of the work itself.

The *Halachot Gedolot* is a codification of Halachah following closely the order of subjects as they are treated in the Talmud, while the language is that of the Talmud itself. Two purposes are therefore served, the first that of acquainting the student with the actual text of the Talmud,

12. Siddur Rav Amram Gaon, p. 38.

13. Ibid.

14. Cf. *Geonica,* p. 111. "The Karaite schism dating from the time of R. Yehudai demanded inexorably a codification of the religious laws affecting practical conduct. The scholar and educated layman alike had to be given the possibility of readily distinguishing the true from the false, the traditional law from the law of the Karaites." Tzernowitz, Toldot Haposskim, vol. 1, p. 72, sees the inclusion of rabbinic precepts in the TaRYaG list of *Halachot Gedolot* as primarily directed against the Karaites and their rejection of the Talmud and its ordinances. *Halachot Gedolot* gives rabbinic ordinances equal status, as it were, with the biblical precept, by including them in his list.

the second that of enabling a practical decision to be reached without plowing through the entire Talmud first. Now one cannot fail to realize that ultimately a TaRYaG enumeration simply amounts to a codification of the principle elements of biblical law. What could therefore be more natural to the first codifier of the Oral Law than to preface his work with a code of the Written Law! The code nature of TaRYaG lies at the very base of every one of the great works on the subject, but nowhere is this stressed more than by the apposition of the biblical code to the first code of the Oral Law by the author of the *Halachot Gedolot*. Understood in this sense, it is in fact a preface in the fullest sense of the word.[15]

There may indeed be a more subtle reason behind the placing of the biblical list of laws before this halachic work.

Already during the time of the Tannaim, the Torah itself had ceased to be used as the textbook for legal discussion. No Tanna looked for the solution to any legal problem in the Torah itself. He searched his knowledge of the Oral Law, as stored either in 'his memory or recorded in the Megilloth Setarim,[16] for material relevant to the problem in hand. It cannot definitely be stated when this replacement of the Mosaic law as the immediate source of decision actually took place, but it was certainly a fact during the second century.[17]

After an interval of five hundred years, R. Acha of Shabcha, the author of the Sheiltot, once again used the Written Law as the starting point for halachic discourse. It is possible that BeHag in placing the biblical code before its

---

15. Cf. the remarks in chap. 4.

16. Cf. Rashi to *Shabbat* 6b and related passages.

17. R. Travers Herford, *Talmud and Apocrypha,* p. 66, following Lauterbach in Midrash and Mishnah, is of the opinion that the changeover commenced with Jose ben Joezer of Zereda a century and a half before the common era. But see the relevant passages in Albeck, *Mevoh LaMishnah* (1959).

talmudic extracts, intended to illustrate unequivocally that the use of he Written Law as the base for Halachic discussion was pointless. All that could be gathered from the biblical code was the bare precept and nothing more. If this is so, we have here the real thrust against the Karaite preoccupation with the Written Law.

The fact is, however, that later scholars took the biblical list as the starting point for their halachic works, with of course the proviso that the Written Law cannot be understood independently from the Tannaitic mishnaic/talmudic base. Thus the problem of "the form of study" eventually turned almost a complete circle. Originally studied as an elaboration of the biblical text, the Oral Law became independent of it and finally became the base for understanding the biblical text itself. In no other branch of rabbinic literature does this cyclical movement become as evident as in the treatment accorded to the TaRYaG tradition over an extended period of more than a thousand years. In the Sheiltoth the original form of study is evidenced, while the *Halachot Gedolot* reverses the process to the mishnaic/talmudic form, and Saadya, Hefez, Maimonides, Semag, and others to the present day examine the biblical text with the Talmud as the starting point.

II

The major problem presented by the enumeration of the *Halachot Gedolot* concerns the division of the precepts, the second problem that of the actual content of the list.

Both BeHag and Saadya Gaon divide the 613 mitvot as follows: 71 capital cases, 277 prohibitions, 200 positive commandments, and 65 parashyot (sections). Indeed, the difficulties presented by this division are such that R. Shimon b.

Zemach Duran was led to declare[18] that its understanding
was beyond him. The division does not seem to follow the
accepted talmudic division of 248 positive precepts and 365
prohibitions. This circumstance is doubly strange since Be-
HaG himself, in the opening paragraph of the preface, faith-
fully records the talmudic division.

Careful analysis of the list shows however that there is
no discrepancy between the numbers of BeHaG's division
and those of the Talmud.[19]

It is obvious that the 71 capital cases are to be considered among the prohibitions, so that in fact we are faced
with three main groups of precepts: 200 positive commandments, 348 prohibitions, and 65 parashyot. It is in fact
the third division, the parashyot, that has caused difficulty
because it has not been fully understood. What is the
function of the parashah?

The proper understanding of the parashah lies in the
heading BeHaG himself gives to this section. It says:

> These are the statutes and judgments that are given
> over to the community.

It is quite clear from this heading that apart from any
internal classification of the precepts that one might choose
to make, one overriding division must be borne in mind,
namely, the clear-cut distinction between those mitzvot that
devolve upon the individual qua individual and those that
apply only to properly constituted authority, the Sanhedrin
or Beth Din, representing the community as a whole. For
example, section 46, "Sanctification of the land, to give the
Levites cities of refuge," can obviously only be put into

---

18. *Zohar Harakiah,* p. 11.
19. For the kernel of what follows, cf. A. S. Traub in his introduction
to the *Halachot Gedolot* (Warsaw, 1874).

effect by properly constituted authority and not by an individual. In other words both BeHaG and Saadya Gaon recognize the *corporate responsibility entailed* in many mitzvot of the Torah.[20]

If one enumerated the precepts contained in the parashyot the number would be close to 160 positive and prohibitive commandments, but this is not the intention at all. The Parashyot are not mentioned for the detailed precepts they contain, for then BeHaG would be guilty of counting many precepts more than once, as well as contradicting his number of 65 parashyot. They are detailed by reason of the special directive to constituted authority, which they contain.

Now if we examine the 65 parashyot in this light, we find that 17[21] of them are prohibitive or preventive and are

---

20. The Azharah of Isaac Algerbeloni follows BeHaG in enumerating parashyot but includes fasting on the Day of Atonement as a parashah. This is certainly an individual and not a corporate obligation. This and similar anomalies led Perle (Preface, end pt. 3) to a different estimation of the parashyot to that outlined in the text.

21. The seventeen are:
   (1) Section 3, on damages, personal injury, etc.
   (2) Section 10, on transgression involving sacred vessels.
   (3) Section 11, on laws of cleanness and uncleanness.
   (4) Section 12, on laws of uncleanness in childbirth.
   (5) Section 13, on laws of uncleanness in leprosy.
   (6) Section 14, on laws of uncleanness in flux, menstruation.
   (7) Section 16, on laws of a woman who is a half-slave.
   (8) Section 17, on laws of uncircumcized fruit.
   (9) Section 18, on laws of blemished animals.
   (10) Section 22, on laws of one who blemishes his fellow.
   (11) Section 47, on laws of a false prophet.
   (12) Section 48, on laws of a perverted city.
   (13) Section 50, on laws of false witnesses.
   (14) Section 56, on laws of a rebellious son.
   (15) Section 57, on laws of marital libel.
   (16) Section 58, on laws of rape and inducement.
   (17) Section 61, on laws of a woman who maims one fighting her husband.

dealt with by the courts as things that ought to be prevented. They involve the public body in prohibitions. If
these 17 are added to the 348 prohibitions already mentioned, the talmudic 365 is achieved.

Similarly, the remaining 48 parashyot all involve positive action[22] on the part of constituted authority; and if
these 48 corporate, positive precepts are added to the 200
positive commandments directed to the individual, the
talmudic 248 is achieved.[23]

It is quite clear therefore that BeHaG in no way ignores the classical talmudic division of the precepts;[24] it
simply enhances it with a far-reaching, logical subdivision,
which after Saadya Gaon and some of the Azharot, seems
to have been virtually ignored by all[25] authorities.

---

22. E.g., sec. 1, the directive to constitute the various courts, sec. 4,
the directive to erect the Tabernacle and its appurtenances. Secs. 41
and 42, attending to the public sacrifices, etc.

23. This is substantiated by the fact the Azharot of Eliahu Hazaken
and Isaac Algerbeloni mingle the appropriate parashyot together with
their enumeration of positive precepts and prohibitions, while Ibn
Gabirol lists the positive parashyot after the positive commandments
and the prohibitive parashyot at the conclusion of his enumeration of
the prohibitions.

24. The remarks of both *Otzar Yisrael,* vol. 6 ed. 1911, p. 278, and
Guttman, p. 53, and elsewhere, to the effect that "BeHaG know
nothing of the talmudic division," is seen to be quite groundless. The
fact that BeHaG himself quotes the talmudic division in the preface is
sufficient refutation, while Maimonides, at the end of his preface to the
S.H., declares, "None of those who have listed the mitzvot have been
mistaken concerning this number (viz. 248 and 365)."

25. It is found in Bachya ibn Pakkudei, *Duties of the Heart* (Warsaw,
1875), p. 165. Maimonides, at the conclusion of his list of positive
precepts, mentions that of the precepts there are those that apply to
the community and those that apply to the individual, but the implica-
tion of this fact does not affect his division of the mitzvot. Indeed, he is
prevented from listing the division of "punishments" by the principles
laid down in Root Fourteen. Likewise by the principles in Roots Seven

The nature and importance of the parashyot having been clarified, one is led to inquire whether BeHaG is the originator of this important classification or not. There are two indications that BeHaG is following in this an early rabbinic tradition and is not in fact the inventor of this subdivision.

In the Rome manuscript of the *Halachot Gedolot*, which was edited by Hildersheimer, the preface reads as follows:

The Rabbis taught (Heb. Shanu), 65 parashyot are of the body of Torah, and each of the parashyot was explained by the Sages of Israel.

The prefix "shanu" occurs when a Baraitha is being quoted, and it would therefore seem that BeHaG is quoting a Baraitha that has not survived as the source for the fourfold division that follows.

Evidence that the Rabbis did have a division other than positive and prohibitive commandments is available from the following midrashic[26] source. The passage is quoted in the name of R. Yehuda b. Simon, who, in another passage,[27] gives the conventional division of the mitzvot.

Said the Holy One, Blessed be He, I gave them positive commandments, which they accepted upon themselves, and also prohibitions, which they accepted upon themselves. I did not reveal to them their reward, and they said nothing to Me, and several other mitzvot, therefore. . . .

and Ten he is forced to ignore the "parashyot" classification. The "Chinuch" (see chap. 9) also recognizes the corporate nature of some precepts. Sefer Hachinuch, end para. 95; 107; 397.

26. Midrash Tehillim, ed. Buber (Wilna, 1891), p. 488.

27. *Genesis Rabbah,* chap. 24.

The passage presents a difficulty in that, having cited both positive and prohibitive commandments, what "other mitzvot" remain? It is, however, readily understood if the fourfold grouping of the Geonim is borne in mind. The "other mitzvot" would then be discoverable in the parashyot and punishments, or, if the latter are grouped with the prohibitions, the parashyot only.[28] This deduction from the passage is further indicated by the interjection of "I did not . . . to Me" before "and several other mitzvot," since if the "other mitzvot" are indeed the parashyot, it is understandable why no special point is made of the failure to express bestowal of reward in these instances, for the parashyot are directed to constituted authority and not to the individual.

A final problem concerning the parashyot lies in the origin of this particular title for these mitzvot. Y. P. Perle, in his extensive work on Saadya's *Sefer HaMitzvot*,[29] is of the opinion that the origin of the title parashah is connected with the Hebrew "Parashath Derachim," parting of the ways, since these mitzvot are comprised of both positive and prohibitive commandments. This explanation seems farfetched. Having already fully explained the nature of the parashah, I feel that the reason for their title is to be found in their particular function.

Mitzvah usually entails obligation in the narrow sense, that is, of or toward an individual, whereas the particular obligations involved in the parashyot are corporate and of a

---

28. An inconclusive passage exists in *Ruth Rabbah*, end sec. 2, where a triple division of "punishments, prohibitions, and other mitzvot," is mentioned.

29. In three parts (Warsaw, 1906–1909). It is quoted extensively by the editors of Saadya's Siddur, and the following opinion of his is taken from the Siddur, p. 179. See also n. 20 above. The opinion there referred to is not the same as the one quoted here.

broader nature. For this reason the title mitzvah does not express them as fully as is warranted. Parashah, in rabbinic literature, Tannaitic as well as Amoraic,[30] is used in a wider sense and well expresses the corporate nature of those mitzvot that entail more than the narrow obligation and liability of the individual.

III

To turn now to the second problem of BeHaG's list, that of its content. It is well known that Maimonides' Fourteen Roots are directed primarily against the enumeration of the *Halachot Gedolot*, and indeed, the number of mitzvot on which the two lists differ is considerable.[31] Complete agreement affects only 294 prohibitions and 168 positive commandments. The remaining 151 precepts are made up differently in the two lists. The disagreement prevailing in no less than 26 percent of the precepts leads to the complete divergence of the enumerations.

The great defender of BeHaG against Maimonides' strictures was Nachmanides, whose many works reflect a general attitude of defending established authority.[32] However, in no field more than our own does his essential

30. See Bacher, Terminologie, pt. 1, p. 109–110; and pt. 2, p. 266–267.

31. Of BeHaG's enumeration, sixty-four prohibitions, sixty-five positive commandments, and fifteen of his parashyot do not appear in Maimonides' list. On the other hand, forty-one of Maimonides' prohibitions, not listed separately by BeHaG, appear in the parashyot, eighteen do not appear at all, and in the case of a further ten that do not appear, Nachmanides is in agreement as to their omission. One hundred and twenty-five of Maimonides' positive commandments are included in the parashyot, ten do not appear at all, and in the case of a further eight that do not appear, Nachmanides is in agreement with BaHaG.

32. See Dr. I. Una, *The Life and Works of Moses b. Nachman* (Jerusalem, 1942), chap. 8.

impartiality come to the fore. In spite of his lengthy argument against Maimonides' Root One, he does not hesitate to conclude with "but in spite of all this, the words of Maimonides are closer to us."[33]

To my mind Nachmanides' purpose in entering the lists was twofold. First, BeHaG must have held some opinion on topics that affect the very essence of Torah in the traditional view, but his dry enumeration of the precepts leaves the impression that it was drawn up without care or attention. And second, Nachmanides himself was by no means satisfied with all of Maimonides' conclusions concerning the nature of the law and tradition.[34] The polemic that Maimonides directed against BeHaG simply afforded an arena in which to treat the matter extensively and thoroughly. Whether BeHaG is vindicated or not is beside the point; the search for the theoretical concepts of Halachah provides a broad enough canvas to embrace varying schools of thought. What is important is that the discussion, occasioned by BeHaG's list, places the fundamental concepts of Halachah under the microscope in a manner never previously attempted, nor later equaled. The absolute mastery of the entire rabbinic literature that is arrayed before the student is amazing. The conclusions that emerge illuminate the foundations upon which the entire structure of Halachah is built.

Now it is well to remember that in the early period it was not the custom of the Geonim to *discuss* their halachic

---

33. Perle, preface, pt. 3, notes that several of the differences between Nachmanides and Maimonides concerning BeHaG's list are due to the fact that each had different manuscripts of the *Halachot Gedolot*. Maimonides seems to have had what is now called the Rome manuscript of the *Halachot Gedolot* in his possession.

34. See chap. 2.

decisions. A decision was often rendered with no more than a yes or no. Discussion was a matter for the academies, not for the respondent to convey to his questioner. A halachic compendium to the Geonic mind could only contain the summation of the Halachot involved. The machinery whereby that summation was achieved could only be gained by years in the academies. Certainly the academies, in discussing the methods by which the Halachah is derived from the talmudim, discussed thoroughly all the theoretical problems of Halachah, but no need was felt to commit these discussions to writing. BeHaG's enumeration is doubtless a product of this discussion, and Nachmanides' brilliant work recaptures for us much of the searching enquiry that led to its promulgation.[35]

IV

Saadya Gaon (882–942), without doubt the most colorful literary personality of the Geonic period, wrote extensively on TaRYaG. Apart from the Azharah "Anochi Esh Ochela" ("I am a consuming fire"), in which TaRYaG are

35. While it would be pointless within the framework of this study to analyze further the content of BeHaG's list, one division of opinion concerning Maimonides' very first precept, that of believing in God, leads to an interesting conclusion that is upheld by all scholars. The precept to believe in God does not appear in BeHaG's list, while Maimonides bases the precept on the first statement of the Decalogue (cf. commentary of S. R. Hirsch to this verse). But although the Bible says in Deuteronomy 4:13, that the Decalogue is "Ten Words," this is not taken by any of those who enumerate TaRYaG to mean that the Decalogue contains only ten precepts. No objection on this score can therefore be raised against BeHaG for omitting the first statement of the Decalogue from his list of precepts. Maimonides lists fourteen precepts as being contained in the Decalogue, S.H. positive commandments 1, 155, 210; and prohibitions 1, 2, 5, 6, 62, 265, 289, 285, 243, 320, and 347.

enumerated according to their relationship with the ten statements of the Decalogue,[36] he compiled a lengthy Piyyut[37] in which TaRYaG are divided, as in the *Halachot Gedolot*, into 200 positive precepts, 277 prohibitions, 71 capital cases, and 65 parashyot.

But in addition to this broad classification of the mitzvot, the groups of precepts are further subdivided. Thus in the middle of the first group, that of positive commandments, we read:

> These ninety-seven precepts continually complete
> For precepts of the body are they, learn them well,
> delight in them, and you will surely reap
> Well, the produce that I have treasured up, giving
> it forth to those who trust, saying,
> Because in my ways you walk, my statutes and ordinances keep.

A clear distinction is here made between those mitzvot that are independent of possession of the holy land, Chovoth Hagguff, and those that are dependent upon residence, and in some instances possession, of the holy land.

In concluding the mitzvot that refer to the various sacrifices and the directives to the priests, he says:

> Thus shall you Bless, and this is your statute, fifty-eight precepts complete.

And finally, having listed the precepts involved in ritual impurity in its varied forms, he concludes:

---

36. See chap. 4. For a technical discussion of the style of Saadya's Azharot, see Malter, p. 150 and notes ad loc. p. 152, p. 331, no. 3.

37. On the relationship between these two works see Perle, preface, sec. 11.

Concluding the precepts forty-five, separations from impurity drawing nigh.

The prohibitions are likewise subdivided into groups of 142 and 135. Then follow the various capital crimes. But although Saadya agrees with BeHaG in listing 71 types of capital offenses, he has 7 classes of capital crime to Be-HaG's 6. He includes that of punishment by the Zealot when caught in the act.[38] In order to fit in the two[39] extra cases involved, namely, stealing a sacred vessel and making an Aramean his paramour, he is forced to omit 2 of the capital instances enumerated by BeHaG.

Next follow the sixty-five parashyot, which are also subdivided into two groups, one of forty sections and the other of twenty-five. These latter refer mainly to aspects of public sacrifice, priestly functions, temple and appurtenances, the Levites, etc.

These internal divisions greatly lighten the task of ascertaining Saadya's enumeration, for it must be remembered that the actual Azharah and Piyyut contain no divisions between the mitzvot at all. The strophes simply follow one another without pause or break, and a discerning eye is required to determine the number of precepts in each strophe. Even an apparently simple strophe poses its problems. One is left wondering whether, for example, "Her food, raiment, and marital due in proper time," is intended to be one precept[40] or two [41] or perhaps even

---

38. Sanhedrin, 82a. Cf. Rashi to Numbers 25:7–8.

39. These cases are mentioned in the Mishnah, *Sanhedrin* 9:6. It is difficult to understand why Saadya lists two of the cases mentioned in the Mishnah and omits the third, which is actually stated between the other two.

40. As in Maimonides, prohibition 62, and SeMaG, prohibition 81.

41. As in SeMaK 276, 277.

three. Two modern editions of Saadya's work are available in which great strides are made to ascertain exactly Saadya's TaRYaG list. Neither is free from criticism.[42]

Saadya also wrote a treatise dealing with only a section of the mitzvot, those called "Shemuot"[43] which has not been preserved.[44]

Among the bibliographical lists of Saadya's works, one item in particular caused a furor among scholars for many years. It was listed under four different titles, and since it was entirely unavailable in any form, it gave rise to multiple conjecture. The *Sefer HaMitzvot* of Saadya Gaon was thought variously to be a polemical work on the mitzvot, a recension of Saadya's *Book of Doctrines and Beliefs*, his introduction to the Talmud, etc. Dr. Z. Banat, in

---

42. S. Halpern published an edition in 1930 (Jerusalem). It is, however, devoted mainly to ascertaining which of Maimonides' Fourteen Roots Saadya concurs. He concludes that Saadya agrees with Roots 1, 4, 5, 8, 10, 11, and 13 unreservedly but that he agrees with Roots 2 and 12 only with qualifications. Concerning Roots 3, 6, 7, 9, and 14, they disagree. The major edition, used by the editors of Saadya's Siddur, is in three volumes and is an extensively detailed work on the enumeration itself. It was first published by Y. P. Perle (Warsaw, 1906–1909). Perle concludes that Saadya disagrees completely with Maimonides' Roots 4, 6, 13, and 14, and, while agreeing with the remaining roots, these are all subject to moderation and qualification. This opinion is to be preferred to that of Halpern. The divergence of opinion concerning the roots and their interpretation is responsible for the omission by Saadya of no less than 84 positive commandments and 120 prohibitions enumerated by Maimonides. They are listed by Perle, preface, pp. 46–49.

43. Literally, "Those that are heard," referring to those precepts that man's unaided reason would not have evolved. Dr. Banat, in *Saadya Memorial Volume 1942*, p. 366 n. 8, is of the opinion that the word is borrowed from Moslem usage, the Moslems having received even their Written Law, the Koran, by "hearing" it from Mohammed.

44. See Dr. Banat, pp. 336–370. Also, *Toledot Haposekim*, S. M. Chones (New York, 1946), p. 462, c. 2, no. 23.

his important study of the problem, published in the
Saadya Memorial Volume 1942,[45] examines and upsets all
of these theories. He establishes without doubt the fact
that Saadya wrote an extensive work in Arabic on TaRYaG,
in which all of the mitzvot were carefully enumerated and
described, while the biblical verse from which each mitzvah is drawn was stated at the conclusion of the discussion
of the mitzvah.[46]

The work was prefaced by an introduction[47] that classified the mitzvot, which has been preserved largely by
means of an exposition of R. Shemuel b. Chofni Gaon.[48] His
system of enumerating the mitzvot is fully expounded both
in the preface and in the treatment of the individual mitzvot. The first paragraph of Banat's translation reads as
follows:

The head of the college, al-Fayyumi, may God shine
upon his face, divided them in the Reshut (introduction) to the Azharah into twenty-five sections, which
we will enumerate briefly in Arabic, although he
listed them in Hebrew, without mentioning all of the
mitzvot but only some of them.

The paragraph concludes with "and many of them are
mentioned above," which indicates that the fragment is

---

45. "The Beginning of the *Sefer HaMitzvot* of Rav Saadya," pp.
365–381.

46. See *Toledot Haposekim*, p. 463, c. 1, no. 26. Also Assaph, p. 193,
who gave the original fragments of the work to Dr. Banat. Further
fragments were found in the Geniza treasures at Cambridge and at the
Rabbinical Seminary of New York.

47. Published originally in Arabic by Neubauer, *Jewish Quarterly
Review* 6: 705–707, and translated into Hebrew by Banat, pp. 378–381.

48. See Banat, p. 371 n. 33.

part of a *Book of Precepts*. Then follow the twenty-five classes into which the precepts are divided. The fragment, however, breaks off after the twenty-first section.

From what has been said, it will be seen that Saadya's work on TaRYaG was indeed extensive. He covered the ground from the popular Azharah on the one hand to the detailed study of principles on the other. Halper's remarks[49]—"It may thus be said that there are three main systems of enumerating the precepts: (1) that of the author of the *Halachot Gedolot*, (2) that of Chefetz b. Yatzliach, and (3) that of Maimonides"—are seen to be mistaken. In view of the Sefer HaMitzvot of Saadya here discussed, there is at least a fourth system.[50]

Unfortunately it is not possible to gauge the influence of Saadya's work in this field. His Azharot entered no liturgy, and the fact that his major work was written in Arabic precluded its widespread use by the centers rising in the West. When the Tibbonites gave European Jewry access to their Arabic treasures, Maimonides already dominated the scene.[51]

V

One of the most prolific of the Geonic writers was R. Shemuel b. Chofni, Gaon of Sura 997–1013. About thirty of his works are known and among them is a *Sefer Ha-*

---

49. *Jewish Quarterly Review* 4 (April 1914): 525.

50. The S.H. of R. Shemuel b. Chofni, apart from its particular method of grouping the precepts, is probably modeled as to their enumeration on Saadya's work, as is shown by his lengthy quotation of Saadya's preface.

51. On the fact that Rashi, who knew no Arabic, knew Saadya's Azharot. Comm. to Exodus 24:12), see H. Malter, *Life and Works of S. Gaon*, p. 287 and n. 626 ad loc.; and p. 290 and n. 638.

Mitzvot. Mention has already been made of the strong connection and influence that Saadya's *Sefer HaMitzvot* had upon him, and his originality in this field is confined solely to the arrangement of the mitzvot. He is not, however, a slavish follower of Saadya's work and he differs from several of the latter's categories in his division of the mitzvot. He would, however, hardly have preserved for us Saadya's complete system of classification if he were not in the main in agreement with it.

VI

The few known biographical details of Chefetz b. Yazliach are thoroughly examined by Halper in his edition of the Arabic manuscript of Chefetz's *Sefer HaMitzvot*.[52] Until the discovery of the manuscript, the work was known only from scattered references. However, Bahya ibn Pekudah's reference to it[53] illustrates the esteem in which the work was held, since Bahya mentions only an extremely select list of current authoritative works on various branches of Jewish law and thought.

From Maimonides' preface to his *Sefer HaMitzvot*[54] we know that Chefetz severely criticized the TaRYaG enumerations of his predecessors. But apart form criticizing the manner of their enumeration, he seems also to have been dissatisfied with their manner of presentation. In departing from both the manner and content of their works,

---

52. *Jewish Quarterly Review*, ibid.

53. *Duties of the Heart*, introduction.

54. Heller, p. 3 and n. 29. Also Sede Chemed, vol. 3. ed. Warsaw. Kellallei Haposkim, Oth HEH, no. 21. Chefez criticized mainly Be-HaG's list. The criticism must have been contained in the lengthy introduction (quoted by Chefez in the preserved fragment, folio 17a) to the work, of which nothing survives.

Chefetz gives a lengthy[55] discussion of each detail of the mitzvot, to the extent that his work provides the first known attempt to codify talmudic law in its entirety in Arabic.

The book follows an arrangement particular to the author. All the precepts, positive and prohibitive, belonging to one category are in one book[56] and are then subdivided into sections according to subject matter. The exhaustive analysis by Halper of the preserved fifty-one precepts shows that in thirty of them Maimonides is in agreement with his predecessor, while the remainder are excluded by Maimonides' Roots Seven and Twelve. Halper concludes that Root Seven in particular seems to have been directed against Chefetz.[57]

Though primarily a halachist, Chefetz deals exhaustively with the philosophical and ethical facets of the mitzvot. It seems that he was equally concerned with the metaphysical aspects of Judaism as with Halachah. In this approach he anticipates Maimonides himself, whose atti-

---

55. A point that escaped even Halper's notice (ibid., p. 546) is the fact that in all the editions of the *Duties of the Heart,* the S.H. of Chefez is described as giving a brief account of the mitzvot. Study of the preserved manuscript indicates that the probable length of the work was about a thousand pages (Halper, ibid., p. 560), and the treatment of the mitzvot in the preserved sixty-three pages is anything but brief. How then could Bahya, who was evidently acquainted with the work, so describe it? The fault lies in a mistranslation of Bahya's Arabic text. Ziphronis' translation, on the basis of several Arabic manuscripts (Tel Aviv, 1950, p. 70), reads, "And the second type of work is that which deals with the essence of the mitzvot either briefly or fully as the work of Chefez b. Yatzliach."

56. The number of books in the entire work is not known. Chefez himself, however, quotes the thirty-sixth book.

57. But as pointed out above, n. 42, Saadya also disagrees with Maimonides' Root Seven.

tude to Halachah, as shown in his commentary to the Mishnah[58] and in the first book of the Yad Hachazakkah,[59] also embraces the ethical and metaphysical aspects of Judaism.

58. *Berakhot* 9:5.
59. *Yesodei HaTorah,* which deals exclusively with the philosophical and metaphysical bases of Torah.

6

Maimonides' *Sefer HaMitzvot* (Part One)

I

The *Sefer HaMitzvot* of Maimonides[1] represents both the turning point and culmination in the study of TaRYaG. With one possible exception, the Sepher Yeraim by R. Eliezer of Metz, no TaRYaG work written after the twelfth century fails to take cognizance of the *Sefer HaMitzvot*. The study of TaRYaG is at once broadened in scope and

---

1. Written in 1170, S.H. has been published in numerous editions. Moise Bloch (Paris, 1888) published the Arabic text with notes. A critical Hebrew edition, based on the translation of Ibn Tibbon but comparing this translation with those of Ibn Iyyob, Ibn Chisdai, and various manuscripts of the Arabic text as well as the works that quote the S.H. was published by Ch. Heller, 2nd rev. ed. (New York, 1946). Such was the popularity of the work that it was translated into Latin (S. Zeitlim, *Maimonides: A Biography*

limited in extent by Maimonides' work. The major difference between the pre– and post–Maimonidean study of
the subject may be considered in the relationship of scholarly work. In the pre–Maimonidean period work was
based on faulty, incomplete manuscripts. After Maimonides scholarly work was undertaken on the basis of
collated and authoritative texts.

The freedom and conjecture of the pre–Maimonidean
authors is entirely absent from the work of later scholars. A
single name and a single work dominates the field.

We have already examined the contribution of both the
Azharot[2] and the Geonim[3] to the concept of TaRYaG. The
Azharot represent the development of rabbinic theories concerning the Decalogue, while the works of the Geonim
develop the halachic theory of TaRYaG. These two fields
represent in fact the sum of the concepts underlying TaRYaG.
One searches in vain for any additional basic approach to the
subject. Neither Maimonides[4] nor his successors added to this
concept. Nevertheless the *Sefer HaMitzvot* is recognized, and
rightly so, as the basic work on the subject.

The reason is not hard to find. Consider Maimonides'
Mishneh Torah. It contains little in material or content that
is new.[5] Its tremendous impact upon Halachah and halach-

[New York, 1935], p. 221 n. 36); into Italian (see Jellineck, Kontras TaRYaG
no. 17); into French by M. Bloch (Paris, 1888), and into German (printed in
Hebrew characters) under the title *Chok-Leyisrael* (Prague, 1798). It was
published anonymously; the initials I. E. L. appear on the title page in
place of the author's name. Jellineck, Kontras TaRYaG no. 56 identifies the
author as Israel Halevi Landau.

2. Chapter 4.
3. Chapter 5.
4. See chap. 5 of this study.
5. We have already shown, chap. 6, that even the thought underlying *Yesodei HaTorah* is found in the work of Chefez.

ists is due to the analysis, structure, presentation, form, and style with which it invests the Halachah, rather than in newness. The old has received a new face, but it is still the selfsame ancient Halachah. This approach is characteristic of Maimonides' work as a whole. The originality of his commentary to the Mishnah lay in the analytical method of interpretation that is the base of the commentary. The *Mishneh Torah* relies for originality on the scientific edifice of Halachah that Maimonides succeeds in erecting. Similarly, the originality of the *Sefer HaMitzvot* lies in the analysis and presentation of accepted canons. Penetrating analysis and a passion for systemization, together with a highly developed critical ability and a phenomenal mastery of all branches of Torah, are responsible for the redaction and recasting of rabbinic literature in Maimonides' hands, but he is governed throughout by the ancient, prevailing concepts of his material, the Halachah.

Maimonides' treatment of Halachah in *Mishneh Torah* achieves two basic purposes. *Mishneh Torah* must never be considered as simply containing unending lists of Halachot. The Halachot are so arranged that the organic development of any Halachah from the biblical text unto his own day is clearly shown. The unity of Torah and its natural development are clearly shown. Second, there emerges from *Mishneh Torah* as a whole a total view of Judaism as a guide to life. These two facts alone give unparalleled stature to *Mishneh Torah*.

Mishneh Torah flows smoothly. The labor involved in the analysis to which the entire Oral Law has been subjected in order to create it passes unnoticed. The extraction of principles from the mass of halachic detail, in order to clarify the methods used in the talmudim to arrive at decisions, thus enabling Halachah to expand on the basis of those methods, required skill, depth, acumen, and masterly collation of references scattered through thousands of folio pages of literature, yet nowhere in *Mishneh Torah* do we have so much as a hint of the thought processes that resulted in its creation.

It is in the *Sefer HaMitzvot* alone that one is presented with a masterly précis of the halachic process that underlies each statement of *Mishneh Torah*.

Argument and refutation, the dynamics that constitute the very lifeblood of Halachah,[6] are absent in *Mishneh Torah*, which, because of its departure from accepted methods of presenting Halachah, was thought to constitute a grave danger to the Halachah it attempted to serve.[7] With

---

6. To Maimonides' remarks in his preface to *Mishneh Torah* to the effect that "I have called this code *Mishneh Torah* because a person may read the Written Law first and then read in this book and know from it the entire Oral Law without studying any intermediate work," Ra'aBaD comments, "His (Maimonides') intention was constructive but it has failed to be so, for he has forsaken the method of all previous codifiers who brought proofs for their decisions and quoted their authorities, from which practice great benefit was derived. For it often happens that the Dayyan, relying upon a certain authority, decides to permit or prohibit; if however he had known that there exists a more important source, he would have decided in its light, and now I do not know why I should leave my received decision and proof for the sake of this compiler. If he who disagrees with me is greater than I, all well and good, but if I be greater than he, why should I annul my reasoning for his? And furthermore, there are matters concerning which the Geonim argue with one another, and this compiler chose to decide according to the one opinion and included it in his code. Why should I rely upon his choice if I do not agree with it? And (I am at a disadvantage because) I know not who is his opponent, whether it is fitting to argue with him or not." See also responsa of Rabbenu Asher, Klall 31, 9.

7. Moses Hagiz, in his work dealing with qualities by which the Torah is acquired (enumerated in *Ethics of the Fathers,* chap. 6) comments on the apparent violence of Ra'aBaD's strictures against Maimonides as follows; "When this great and wonderful work appeared . . . closed and sealed as if given by Moses from Sinai, whereas in truth

Maimonides, normal halachic procedure finds its place in the *Sefer HaMitzvot,* where he argues with and refutes the opinions of his predecessors,[8] forestalls questions,[9] quotes biblical and rabbinic sources[10] in abundance, as well as his own works[11] and opinions,[12] establishes correct readings of

---

it contains many statements that the great and learned of Israel have disputed and still dispute, Ra'aBaD was afraid lest coming generations would follow Maimonides automatically and would be afraid to argue against the decision of the Master, thinking it to be the unanimous decision of all scholars . . . and will not turn from his words to the right or to the left. Therefore, to remove this stumbling block from later generations of scholars, Ra'aBaD, although in the main agreeing with Maimonides, girded up his loins and showed that where the decision of Israel's scholars is not in accordance with that expressed in the Yad, it is permitted to argue against Maimonides." (Hebrew text quoted in *Sinai,* January 1955.) There was also the danger that people would use the code blindly and decide matters of law without understanding them properly. In this connection the Talmud itself pronounces against those who render decisions on the basis of the Mishnah alone (*Sotah* 22a and Rashi ad loc.).

8. In the roots, the author of *Halachot Gedolot,* Chefez b. Yatzliach, and the authors of the Azharot are specifically confronted.

9. Positive commandments 57, 75, 77, 82, 117, 187. Prohibitions 9, 143, 168, 170, 187, 272.

10. The biblical source is quoted to every precept. Maimonides is, however, sparing in his quotation from the remaining books of the Bible. The following are the only quotations from the prophetic Books. 1 Samuel 15:2, in positive commandment 189; 1 Kings: 8:44. positive commandment 5; 1 Kings 18:28, prohibition 45; Isaiah 29:22, positive commandment 9; Ezekiel 44:20, prohibition 163; Joel 3:1; Amos 9:11, in the preface Micah 2:2, prohibition 266; Zephaniah 1:8, prohibition 30; and Malachi 2:11, prohibition 51. At the end of the work, Psalms 19:9. Rabbinic sources are quoted in every root and to every precept; they are from Mishnah, Tosephta, Mechilta, Sifra, Sifre, both talmudim, Mishnath R. Eliezer, and various midrashim.

11. Positive commandments 31, 46, 55, 69, 108. Prohibitions 133, 336, 353, etc.

12. Positive commandments 150, 153, 287. Prohibitions 13, 42, 43, 44, 46, 66, 232, etc.

texts,[13] justifies both the inclusion of positive[14] and prohibitive[15] commandments and the exclusion of others,[16] and deals at unusual length with many[17] mitzvot. Here the Master is at work in the halachic laboratory, and it is significant that Maimonides' keenest critic, Ra'aBaD,[18] had never seen the *Sefer HaMitzvot*,[19] owing to the fact that it was written in Arabic.

Maimonides, who was the first halachic author ever to write a preface that explains the nature and scope, as well as the reason, for a work, introduces his *Sefer HaMitzvot* with a fairly long preface.

An important fact, which seems to have escaped the attention of scholars, is that the preface is as much an introduction to *Mishneh Torah* as it is to the *Sefer HaMitzvot*. In addition to illustrating the inherent connection between the two works[20] in Maimonides' mind, the preface seems to me to offer a solution to the baffling problem of the language used in the *Sefer HaMitzvot*.

---

13. Prohibition 199, etc.

14. 9, 20, 38, 66, 87, 149, 213, 218.

15. 194, 206, 333, 349.

16. Positive commandments 20, 56, 89, 93, 209.

17. Positive commandments 9, 20, 37, 56, 73, 111, 153, 176, 187, 209. Prohibitions 5, 6, 10, 31, 32, 60, 61, 63, 72, 89, 90, 94, 153, 161, 165, 170, 179, 181, 187, 214, 237, 242, 247, 266, 290, 293, 317, 336, 347, 352, 353.

18. See n. 6 this chapter.

19. See Heller, preface, p. 2. The fact that the S.H. was not as widely known as it deserved to be is bemoaned by Maimonides himself, responsa 368. It is also the reason the problem of the sources of *Mishneh Torah* baffled scholars. Had the S.H. been widely known, the abundant use of sources in the S.H. would have eased this problem considerably. Maimonides himself wished later to translate the work into Hebrew.

20. I have elsewhere attempted to show that the commentary to the Mishnah, the *Sefer HaMitzvot*, and the *Mishneh Torah* form in fact a halachic trilogy.

The last paragraph of the first part of the preface, which deals with *Mishneh Torah*, reads as follows:

> Because of this my purpose, I arrived at the conclusion that it would be fitting to place at the beginning of the work a list of all the precepts, positive and prohibitive, so that the work may be divided under their headings and also so that no mitzvah may escape my attention. . . . In order to ensure that nothing is missed out and not dealt with, it is necessary to enumerate them and state that, for example, the laws concerning idolatry embrace so many positive mitzvot and they are such and such, and so many prohibitions, namely, such and such. By enumerating the mitzvot, I am safe from omission.

From this it is obvious that Maimonides had no intention of compiling a work devoted solely to the subject of TaRYaG. In fact, it seems from what he next says,

> After this had become clear to me, and I attempted to compile the work (i.e., *Mishneh Torah*), and enumerate all the mitzvot explicitly at the beginning,

that he actually commenced[21] writing *Mishneh Torah,* and only because he was unable to carry out his plan of listing

---

21. The responsa to Tzor, Friemann, no. 368—in which Maimonides states, "There is a work that I compiled before this one (*Mishneh Torah*), which I called *Sefer HaMitzvot*"—does not deny that he commenced *Mishneh Torah* first. In any event, the first half of this preface, which contains a laborious explanation of the plan and style of *Mishneh Torah,* clearly shows that he had devoted considerable thought to *Mishneh Torah* before conceiving the necessity for the *Sefer HaMitzvot.*

the mitzvot successfully did he have recourse to TaRYaG. Since he had already decided, as he himself informs us in this preface, to compile *Mishneh Torah* in Hebrew, it is strange that he reverted to Arabic for the *Sefer HaMitzvot*. It is unusual, to say the least, for an introductory work to be written in a different language from the major work that is to follow.

Bearing in mind the intended scope of *Mishneh Torah,* as declared by Maimonides both in this preface and in the preface to *Mishneh Torah,* to have been that

One should need, besides the written Torah itself, no other book in order to know anything one may need to know appertaining to Torah, whether of biblical or rabbinic origin,[22]

and Maimonides' declared intention of avoiding all reference to sources, sages, and scholars, to anything, in fact, that would render any statement in the work controversial, the following solution suggests itself.

Maimonides saw *Mishneh Torah* as the guide embodying accepted Halachah in every possible field. There was to be no doubt in the mind of the Jew as to what Halachah taught in a given instance.[23] For this reason, alternative opinions or discussion had no place in the work. Similarly,

---

22. Scholars have debated the seriousness of Maimonides' intention in this connection. All have failed to notice the similar expression that appears in the *Sefer HaMitzvot* positive commandment 108, where he says, "And we have explained this order (Tohoroth) completely, in such a manner that one need study no other book in connection with the laws of impurity." CF. also his remarks at the conclusion of Hilchot Kiddush Hachodesh, 19, 16.

23. An exception, where Maimonides himself remained in doubt, is found in Hilchot *Sanhedrin,* chap. 4, Hal. 11.

the TaRYaG list at the head of the work, as that before each section of the work, was to be a simple enumeration of TaRYaG headings. Maimonides was not able to work out the TaRYaG list without publishing his reasons,[24] so he was forced to publish the *Sefer HaMitzvot*. To have allowed this work to become joined to *Mishneh Torah*, as its rightful introduction, would have defeated the very purpose of *Mishneh Torah*. Since the *Sefer HaMitzvot*, being a halachic discourse of magnitude, would have invited discussion and argument (as it later did in any case), it therefore had to be separated from *Mishneh Torah*. This separation was achieved by writing it in Arabic.

II

Post–Maimonidean authors devoted far more attention to the first part of the *Sefer HaMitzvot*, that is to the Fourteen Roots, than they did to the actual TaRYaG list contained in the second part of the work. So important was the first part of the work considered that it came to be called a "Shass Kattan" (i.e., a miniature Talmud), by later scholars.[25] No discussion of the *Sefer HaMitzvot* would therefore be complete without some consideration of this most difficult part of the work. Before dealing with the problems surrounding the actual enumeration of Maimonides, an attempt will here be made to discuss the roots as briefly as possible,

---

24. He explains in the preface that the subject of TaRYaG had become so popularized by the Azharot that were he to publish a different list than those embodied in the current Azharot, without proving the rectitude of his divergence from them, he would have been considered as mistaken and virtually ignored.

25. See J. J. Kalenberg, *Seder HaMitzvot* (1861), preface. Moses Hagiz, Eyleh Hamitzvoth, end of Root Nine.

together with some of the major problems to which they give rise.[26]

The *First Root* states: "It is wrong to include in this number rabbinic injunctions." Maimonides in discussing this root declares that since R. Simlai himself states[27] that "613 precepts were told to Moses at Sinai," it is obvious that rabbinic ordinances are not to be included. He is nevertheless forced to deal with the problem of rabbinic ordinances since, without exception, his predecessors did include them in their TaRYaG lists.

The major problem to which Maimonides' discussion gives rise in this root is that of the measure of culpability in the transgression of a rabbinic ordinance. The Torah states:[28]

According to the law that they shall teach thee, and according to the judgment that they shall tell thee, thou shalt do; thou shalt not turn aside from the matter that they tell thee, to the right hand nor to the left.

The Sifre deduces from here both a positive and a prohibitive commandment to listen to the decrees and ordinances of the teachers of the Torah.[29] Maimonides[30] is of the opinion that one who fails to carry out the decree of the Sages transgresses not only the particular rabbinic

---

26. Perle, preface, pt. 6, shows clearly the indebtedness of Maimonides to Ibn Ezra in the formulation of several of the roots. Maimonides, however, nowhere mentions Ibn Ezra in this connection.

27. See the first page of this study.

28. Deuteronomy 17:11.

29. See S.H. positive commandment 174, prohibition 312. Cf. also chap. 2 n. 33.

30. Mamrim, chap. 1, Hal. 2.

ordinance but also the biblical prohibition contained in this verse.[31] Nachmanides and others oppose this view.[32]

Other authorities[33] consider that according to Maimonides the prohibition refers only to one who rebels against the authority vested in the Sages by this verse, but the infringement of a rabbinic ordinance in itself, without the intention to rebel, carries no biblical penalty.

An interesting compromise-understanding of Maimonides' opinion is that of Moses de Trani.[34] This is to the effect that in fact all rabbinic ordinances fall under this prohibition (agreement with the first opinion), but the Sages themselves set a condition that only when one transgresses their word in a rebellious manner (second opinion) does one incur the biblical punishment.[35]

Further points raised by discussion of the root involve an analysis of the concepts of "Reshut" (voluntary obligation) and "Chovah" (bounden obligation), argument concerning individual mitzvot as to whether they are of

31. According to Torah Temimah to this verse, this applies only when the ordinance was promulgated by the court sitting in the Chamber of Hewn Stone. Cf. Chajes' note to *Shabbat* 3b. But Yad Halevi n. 24 considers that any of the places where the High Court sat carry the same distinction. A further condition is mentioned by Malbim to this verse. Some authorities consider that Nachmanides is in agreement with Maimonides when the first condition is fulfilled. However, not all authorities accept these conditions as necessary according to Maimonides.

32. In his Hassagot to this root, Nachmanides upholds the opinion that the prohibition applies only to those laws deduced and promulgated by the Rabbis in accordance with the thirteen hermeneutic rules of interpretation.

33. Lev Sameach to this root; R. M. A. Amiel, Derekh Hakodesh, Shema'atsa One, p. 6. Nachsheveth Moshe to this root, etc.

34. *Kiryat Sefer* (Venice, 1776). Quoted also by Mishneh LeMelech, Mamrim, chap. 1, Hal. 2, and MaHaRaM Shick, precept 496.

35. See also Netzach Yisrael, I. Buberque (Frankfurt, 1816), p. 17.

biblical or rabbinic origin or not. One such example concerns the recital of the Hallel, in which case Nachmanides,
Duran, Daniel HaBabli, and others uphold the contention
of the author of the Halachot that its recital is biblical,
against Maimonides, who holds it to be of only rabbinic
origin.[36] Great importance attaches to Maimonides' statement that any decree, even when promulgated at the
instance of a prophet, is only considered as rabbinic.

The *Second Root* states:

> No law deduced by means of the Hermeneutic Rules
> by which the Rabbis interpreted the Torah is to be
> included in TaRYaG.

We have already dealt at sufficient length with this root in
chapter 2.

The *Third Root* states:

> It is wrong to include in TaRYaG those mitzvot that
> were not enjoined for all time.

Maimonides, in the course of his remarks in this root,
mentions that there are more than three hundred precepts
in the Torah that were enjoined for specific purposes and
times but are not obligatory once the specific occasion had
passed.

Discussion centers mainly on the definition of a "mitzvah Le'shaah" (given for a particular instance or time) and
a precept "Le'Doroth" (one given for all time). Maimonides
himself argues at exceptional length[37] in order to defend
his assertion that the injunction to root out the Seven

---

36. Cf. *Berakhot* 14a, and Tos. and Asheri ad loc.
37. Prohibition 187.

Nations of Canaan[38] is a mitzvah for all time.[39] Other
examples are "And he (the Levite) shall serve no longer,"[40]
and "They shall not go in to see the holy things even for a
moment, lest they die,"[41] Nachmanides holding that these
are precepts for all time.[42]

The *Fourth Root* states:

It is wrong to include commandments that, because of
their general nature, embrace the whole Torah.

Discussion centers upon what is to be considered an all-
embracing mitzvah. Nachmanides lists, "Thou shalt be
perfect with the Lord thy God,"[43] as a particular precept
and the verse, "And in all I command thee shall you be
observant,"[44] as a prohibition, explaining both of these
verses in a manner that makes their object particular.

Maimonides himself faces the difficulty of the precept[45] concerning prayer, since this is only a particular law
of the general precept to serve God.[46]

Problems concerning the relative stringency of positive and prohibitive commandments arise from discussion
of this root,[47] as also the understanding of the term "holy"
as appended to many mitzvot in the Torah.

This root is not to be confused with Root Nine, where
Maimonides is speaking of several injunctions pertaining

----

38. Deuteronomy 20:17.
39. Cf. The precise definition in Sefer Hachinuch, precept 96.
40. Numbers 8:25.
41. Numbers 4:20.
42. See Yad Halevi n. 5.
43. Deuteronomy 18:13.
44. Exodus 23:13.
45. Positive commandment 5.
46. Exodus 23:25. Deuteronomy 13:5.
47. See Yad Halevi n. 5.

to a single mitzvah. Here he is dealing with general statements affecting the whole Torah.

The *Fifth Root* states:

It is wrong to include the reason of a mitzvah as a separate mitzvah.

Occasionally the Torah adds the reason for a mitzvah in the form of a prohibition, for example, "Her former husband, who sent her away, may not take her again to be his wife . . . and thou shalt not cause the land to sin."[48] The several examples of this type of prohibition that are quoted by Maimonides in this root are of basic importance in the study of the reasons for mitzvot generally. Works dealing with the reasons for mitzvot have generally overlooked the biblical reasons contained in the form of prohibitions.

Discussion centers on what is considered to be a reason and what a prohibition.[49] But Nachmanides strikes at the very base of the root by declaring that no prohibition in the Torah is stated *solely* as a reason for a precept. It must also have precept force and come to add something to the previously mentioned precept. The only exception to this is when the prohibition is stated in the form of a positive commandment, for example, "And thou shalt not swear in my name falsely, and thou shalt profane the Name."[50] In this type of case the latter phrase is a reason and not a prohibition.

This difference of opinion naturally gives rise to several important halachic differences between Maimonides

48. Deuteronomy 24:4.
49. Ritvo to *Yoma* 4b quotes examples but apparently had not seen the *Sefer HaMitzvot.* See Heller to this root n. 1.
50. Leviticus 19:12.

and Nachmanides, which are dealt with at length in the commentaries.[51]

The *Sixth Root* states:

In the case of a mitzvah that entails both a positive and a prohibitive commandment, the positive commandment is to be counted with the positive precepts and the prohibition with the prohibitions.

The laws involved in this root fall into three separate classes:

1. Where, in performing a mitzvah, a positive commandment is involved and against neglect of its performance a prohibition is stated, for example, Sabbath observance.[52]

2. Where the prohibition is preceded by a positive commandment, for example, "He may not send her away all his days,"[53] which is preceded by the commandment, "And she shall be his wife."[54]

3. Where the positive commandment follows a prohibition and the prohibition can be rectified by fulfillment of the positive commandment, for example, "Thou shalt not take the dam with the young,"[55] which is followed by "Thou shalt send away the

---

51. Maimonides' opinion receives definite qualification by Yad Halevi, see n. 1 to this root.

52. See S.H. positive commandment 154. Prohibition 320.

53. Deuteronomy 22:29.

54. Ibid.

55. Deuteronomy 22:7.

dam."[56] In all of these types the positive commandment is listed with the positive mitzvot and the
prohibition with the prohibitions.

Nachmanides raises no objection to the principle laid
down insofar as these three instances are concerned, but
he raises the point that there is a fourth type of precept that
contains both a positive commandment as well as a prohibition, which Maimonides ignores. This type is that of the
prohibition that is deduced from a positive commandment.
This type of prohibition is considered many times by the
Talmud[57] to have the force of a positive commandment. All
authorities agree, in fact, that such prohibitions are indeed
considered as positive commandments; they differ as to
whether these are to be included in the TaRYaG list or not.
Megillat Esther, Machshevet Moshe, David Vittal, and Yad
Halevi are of the opinion that Maimonides, in agreement
with the author of the *Halachot Gedolot*, does not include
such cases,[58] whereas Nachmanides does include them.[59]
Nachmanides himself, *Zohar Harakiah*, Kalenberg, and
others are of the opinion that Maimonides does include
them in his enumeration. Perle, in his discussion of Saadya's list,[60] arrives at a strikingly original opinion concerning this type of precept, according to which they are
only considered as positive commandments insofar as
corporal punishment is not administered for their trans-

---

56. Deuteronomy 22:8.

57. *Pesachim* 41a, *Yevamot* 54b, etc.

58. There are, however, certain inconsistencies in Maimonides if
this view is taken and these authorities consider them at length.

59. Although Nachmanides is not entirely consistent in the matter,
see *Seder HaMitzvot* on this root. Cf. also *Zohar Harakiah*, Mitz.
Asseh, no. 82, on this problem.

60. Preface, pt. 3, and on the sixth root, pp. 26–30.

gression. They remain, however, prohibitions, and as such are listed by Saadya.[61]

The *Seventh Root* states:

It is not permitted to include the details pertaining to a commandment.

Both Daniel HaBabli, who was the first to criticize the *Sefer HaMitzvot,* and Nachmanides fail to comment on this root,[62] and their silence has been taken as agreement.[63]

The *Eighth Root* states:

It is wrong to include in the TaRYaG list negative statements together with the prohibitions.

The meaning of this root is that one must avoid listing with the prohibitions statements that simply negate the application of an existing law to the particular instance, for example, "She shall not go out as the slaves go out,"[64] which simply negates the application of an existing law in the case of the Hebrew bondwoman.

---

61. It should also be noted that according to Perle, Saadya Gaon disagreed entirely with this root (see here chap. 5 n. 42). Saadya holds that in such instances only that precept, either the positive or the prohibitive, which is the more embracing in its preceptive force is listed. See Perle to Root Six and on positive precept 1 at length.

62. On the difference between this root and Root Eleven, see the commentary of Lev Sameach.

63. However, as pointed out by Machshevet Moshe, in spite of Nachmanides' silence in the matter the majority of additional precepts listed by him are due to differences over this root. It has already been pointed out (chap. 5 n. 57) that this root seems particularly to have been directed against Chefez b. Yazliach. It would seem that BeHaG, Saadya, Nachmanides, and others disagree in the definition on what is considered a "detail." See Perle at length on this root.

64. Exodus 21:7.

Maimonides, in his lengthy comments to this root, analyzes the terms of negation used by the Torah and points out those terms that the Talmud considers to introduce prohibitions.

Nachmanides agrees with this root with only a single exception, namely, "And he shall not be as Korah."[65] He defines the difference between negations and prohibitions as follows: wherever, without an explicit verse, the matter could be considered forbidden for any reason, the verse is a negation. Where, however, we would have assumed no preventive injunction, the verse is a prohibition.

The *Ninth Root* states:

One cannot include in the TaRYaG list statements embodying a given prohibition or positive commandment; it is the *act* that these statements prohibit or command that is to be included.

This root is the longest among the fourteen, and it embraces many of the fundamental problems of Halachah. However, in opening his discussion of the root, Maimonides devotes some space to a moral, philosophical classification of the precepts of the Torah. He classifies the mitzvot under four headings, which he considers to be the four purposes toward which fulfillment of mitzvot is directed. They are "Deot" (outlook, correct notions), "Peulot" (actions, deeds), "Middot" (ethical habits and characteristics of personality), and "Dibbur" (correct speech, not to misuse the power of speech).[66]

---

65. Numbers 17:5. SeMaG agrees with Nachmanides in this instance.

66. On the relation of these four headings to those used by Maimonides in the Moreh Nevuchim; see Moreh, pt. 3, chap. 31.

The major halachic points of the root are as follows:

1. In those instances where a mitzvah or prohibition is repeated more than once (e.g., Sabbath, twelve times; prohibition against blood, seven times, etc.), the number of repetitions does not increase the number of precepts, unless the Talmud expressly says that a repetition is intended to be an additional precept.

2. When one prohibition includes several subjects, only the one prohibition is counted and not each of the subjects embraced by it. This is called a "Lav SheBiklallot." There are several types of general prohibitions:

(a) For example, "Thou shalt not eat anything with the blood,"[67] which includes among other prohibitions—
Not to eat an animal before its life has departed.[68]
Not to eat the meat of sacrifices before the sprinkling of the blood on the altar.[69]
A court should refrain from food on the day they sentence a criminal to capital punishment,[70] and other cases.[71]

(b) Instances where two things are prohibited and are expressed together under one negative heading, for example, "raw and cooked."[72] These are considered as one prohibition only.

---

67. Leviticus 19:26.
68. *Sanhedrin* 63a.
69. Ibid.
70. Ibid.
71. Ibid.
72. Exodus 12:9.

Maimonides' criterion as to whether a particular prohibition is to be considered as separate or under a general
heading is in the infliction of corporal punishment. If this is
present, the prohibition is separate and is included in
TaRYaG; if not, then it is excluded. Nachmanides rejects
this criterion entirely.

The same reasoning applies in the case of positive
commandments. Where one commandment embraces two
or more details, it is considered as a general precept, for
example, "And thou shalt speak of them"[73] is followed by
"when thou liest down and when thou risest up." Both of
these times are embraced by the former statement and
are therefore to be considered as one mitzvah.[74] Nachmanides disagrees and considers them to be two separate
commandments.[75]

The *Tenth Root* states:

It is wrong to include prefaces that are stated for any
reason.

None of the printed editions of the *Sefer HaMitzvot* contain
any comment by Nachmanides on either this or the following root. All of the commentators on the roots have been
misled into thinking that Nachmanides agrees with these
roots. However, Heller[76] discovered manuscript copy of
Nachmanides' *Sefer HaMitzvot* that contains arguments
against both of these roots as well as additional material on
Root Nine.

---

73. Deuteronomy 6:7.
74. Positive commandment 10.
75. See additional mitzvot of Nachmanides at end of *Sefer HaM-
itzvot.* Also the discussion in Yad Halevi to Root Eleven n. 8.
76. Introduction to second edition. The manuscripts are in the
Seminary Library, New York.

Discussion, and there is little of it, centers around the definition of "Hechsher mitzvah," that which is considered to be preparation for a mitzvah, as opposed to the actual mitzvah itself.

The *Eleventh Root* states:

It is wrong to list the details of a mitzvah separately if, when taken together, they constitute one mitzvah.[77]

This root differs from the preceding one in that its purpose is to analyze those mitzvot that contain many parts (e.g., the four species of the Lulab[78]) in order to ascertain when the infringement of the prohibition "not to diminish,"[79] which applies in the first instance to the parts of a mitzvah,[80] does not take place. It further examines the parts of the mitzvah to discover which, and how many of them, are essential to the performance of the mitzvah (e.g., in the case of Lulab, taking but one of the species is meaningless) or not (as in the case of fringes, where absence of the blue thread[81] does not prevent performance of the mitzvah with the white). The parts are not to be enumerated separately.

The *Twelfth Root* states:

It is wrong to list the different parts of a composite action when in enjoining the action its parts are detailed.

This root differs basically from the previous two roots in that it deals with composite mitzvot, which are made up of

77. See Yad Halevi and *Seder HaMitzvot.*
78. Leviticus 23:40.
79. Prohibition 314.
80. See Rashi to Deuteronomy 12:1, and all enumerators of TaRYaG.
81. Numbers 15:38.

numerous acts, each of which is independent of the other and is connected only by means of the overriding precept. In this case the act itself, being enjoined independently, has meaning and value, but the embracing precept has not been fulfilled, for example, the mitzvah to erect a Sanctuary is stated in the verse, "And they shall make for me a Sanctuary,"[82] but this single mitzvah is completed only by the fulfillment of at least a hundred separate directives concerning the manufacture of the various sections. It is impossible to consider each part a positive commandment since if any one part is lacking, it is the mitzvah concerning the Sanctuary that remains unfulfilled. There can be, for instance, no obligation to make a golden altar[83] unless it is to be part of the Sanctuary.[84] Similarly, the various acts involved in a sacrifice cannot be considered as separate mitzvot.

The principle applies, however, only to the positive injunctions embraced by the mitzvah. It does not refer to the prohibitions[85] since these do not form particulars of the positive commandment. Maimonides has therefore no hesitation in including the prohibition against dividing the bird in the case of the burnt offering[86] as a separate prohibition,[87] although he has already enumerated the service of the burnt offering among the positive commandments.[88]

Nachmanides carries the argument of Maimonides still further and considers the overriding precept in the

---

82. Exodus 25:8.

83. Exodus 30:1–5.

84. Nachmanides, however, considers the manufacture of the Ark to be a separate mitzvah.

85. Mishneh LeMelech, Beth Habechirah, chap. 1, Hal. 15.

86. Leviticus 1:17.

87. Prohibition 112.

88. Positive commandment 63.

case of sacrifices to be simply to sacrifice the various offerings,[89] and he omits Maimonides' positive commandments sixty-three, sixty-four, sixty-five, sixty-six, and sixty-seven as a result.

A further distinction arises that affects the twenty-four gifts given to the priests.[90] The author of the *Halachot Gedolot* listed these gifts as twenty-four separate mitzvot. Maimonides holds that several of these gifts are only particulars of other mitzvot. Thus the hide of the burnt offering,[91] which was given to the priest, forms part of the precept governing the burnt offering. Other instances, such as tithes,[92] he considers to be one mitzvah, embracing both the separation of the tithe from the produce and the delivery of the same to the priest. Nachmanides, however, disagrees and considers

(a) the separation of the heave offering[93]
(b) the separation of *challah*[94]
(c) the separation of the first tithe,[95] and
(d) the separation of the poor tithe[96]

as mitzvot distinct from the act of giving them to the priest.[97] His reason for this is that the act of separation, even if the separated portion is not given to the priest,

---

89. This precept he deduces from Numbers 18:7.

90. *Bava Kamma* 110b. *Chullin* 133b.

91. Leviticus 1:6. The animal was flayed because the hide was not burnt on the altar but given to the priest.

92. Positive commandment 127.

93. Positive commandment 126.

94. Positive commandment 133.

95. Positive commandment 127.

96. Positive commandment 130.

97. He thus replaces the four precepts omitted due to his opinion on sacrifices.

renders the remaining produce free from the prohibition of Tebel[98] and is therefore an independent mitzvah.[99]

The *Thirteenth Root* states:

A mitzvah does not increase in number by virtue of the number of days that it is to be repeated.

Nachmanides fails to comment on this root[100] even to the extent of offering some argument on behalf of the author of the *Halachot Gedolot,* against whom the root is directed.

The *Fourteenth Root* states:

It is wrong to include in the TaRYaG list the number of times a given punishment is ordained.

The point of this root is to establish that only the actual types of punishment enjoined by the Torah, to be inflicted by the court, are to be counted, but not that each time the punishment is inflicted counts as a separate mitzvah. Capital punishment involves therefore one mitzvah for each type.[101] Nachmanides considers the four types to be but details of a single precept, namely, the infliction of capital punishment by the courts.[102]

Even this brief survey of some of the points raised by the roots is sufficient to enable one to realize their embracing and complex nature. A thorough study of them, to-

---

98. Untithed produce, which dare not be eaten.

99. Nachmanides is not quite consistent in this since he ought also to have listed the tithe of the tithe as two mitzvot, positive commandment 129.

100. But see *Zohar Harakiah* on this root.

101. There are four types; see Mishnah *Sanhedrin,* chap. 7.

102. The remaining problems arising from this root are far too numerous to deal with here.

gether with their commentaries, represents in fact nothing less than a fundamental study of the entire body of Halachah together with its underlying concepts.

Nachmanides' criticism of the roots, although possibly undertaken as an apologia for the author of the *Halachot Gedolot*, against whom most of the roots are directed, is in fact as completely an original study of Halachah as is Maimonides' own work. He is faithful only to the Halachah itself and does not hesitate to justify Maimonides when he feels that *Halachot Gedolot* is mistaken.

The definition and acute probing of the fundamental concepts of Halachah that the roots achieve make possible the emergence of a scientific study of Halachah. Without the roots, such a study would be impossible. In this lies their greatest importance, possibly the most important achievement of the entire TaRYaG literature.

One final point before leaving the roots. The pertinent comment on the biblical verses, as sufficiently indicated in this brief survey, show that the roots, together with the detailed treatment of each precept, contained in the second half of the work, forms a halachic commentary on the Pentateuch. It is a pity indeed that this fact has hardly been realized by scholars, for here lies a most penetrating, halachically embracing commentary from the pen of a Master.[103]

---

103. But see Harambam Keparshan Hatorah in Sefer Harambam shel Tarbitz (Jerusalem: Hebrew University Press Association, 1935), pp. 152–163.

7

Maimonides' *Sefer HaMitzvot* (Part Two)

I

The major problem of the *Sefer HaMitzvot* lies in the order of presentation in the TaRYaG list. Chaim Heller[1] expresses himself to the effect that, "in general we do not know the plan whereby Maimonides listed the mitzvot, one following the other," while Rav Tzair[2] expresses his pain and amazement at "the lack of order in the enumeration of Maimonides." How could the "father of order and chief amongst the logicians" allow such an "unfinished product" to proceed from his pen!

Rav Tzair proceeds to base the plan of the *Sefer HaMitzvot* on a statement of Maimonides in the *Guide to the Perplexed*. Maimonides, in discussing the reasons for

---

1. Note 17 to prohibition 49.
2. Bitzaron (1943), pp. 346–354.

the mitzvot, says there[3] that the purpose of the mitzvot "depends upon three things: opinions, morals, and social conduct." Rav Tzair divides the *Sefer HaMitzvot* in accordance with these three principles and finds it difficult to force the precept list into this classification.

He seems to have lost sight of two important facts. The first, that Maimonides only commenced writing the *Guide* eleven years (1181) after the *Sefer HaMitzvot* was completed (1170), and it therefore could not have served as the working plan for the *Sefer HaMitzvot*. And second, if the TaRYaG list is indeed based upon moral premises, why should Maimonides have forsaken the fourfold moral classification that he himself outlines in Root Nine of the *Sefer HaMitzvot* itself[4] for a threefold division that he does not mention at this early stage? Why, it might further be asked, do the lists of the Moreh and the *Sefer HaMitzvot* follow different arrangements when, according to Rav Tzair, they are based on a single plan?

The entire attempt of Rav Tzair cannot therefore be considered as a solution to this problem.

That Maimonides did enumerate TaRYaG according to some definite system is evidenced by three facts.

First, he himself writes when discussing the precepts that are obligatory at the present time,[5] "and these precepts are according to the *order* in which we have arranged them in this list," from which it appears that the arrangement is not a haphazard one.

Second, in a responsum,[6] he himself explained the arrangement and link between several individual precepts.

---

3. Part 3, chap. 31.
4. See the previous chapter on this root.
5. End of the section dealing with the positive commandments.
6. Number 368.

Third, since the *Sefer HaMitzvot* is, as we have already discussed, an introduction to the *Mishneh Torah*, the
arrangement of the list must, to have been useful, have
some affinity with the arrangement in the latter work.

It is, to my mind, this last fact that must provide the
key to the arrangement of the list in the *Sefer HaMitzvot*.
Maimonides himself lists at the end of his preface to *Mishneh Torah* the TaRYaG headings exactly as they are listed
in the *Sefer HaMitzvot*, which, if it proves anything at all,
shows the inherent connection between the two works.

One fact is apparent. Although groups of mitzvot do
actually follow the order in which the mitzvot appear in
the Torah,[7] the list as a whole is not based on the biblical
order of the precepts. This again points to *Mishneh Torah*,
which is based primarily upon, and whose sections follow
a particular arrangement of, the Oral Law.

It is possible to see the internal bond and progression
between several precepts,[8] but this internal link plays only a
limited part in the overall plan of the list. It is responsible for
the bringing together of widely dispersed precepts but not for
the arrangement of the groups themselves. The actual groups
themselves are, of course, of basic importance for *Mishneh
Torah*, which was to follow. However, even the groupings of
the individual mitzvot are not always similar in both works.
Thus, for example, the blessing of the priests appears in

---

7. Positive commandments 4–7, 57–59, 64–66, 115–117, 232–234,
237–242. Prohibitions 17–21, 34–38, 86–88, 133–135, 141–149,
158–160, 163–165, 172–174, 189–191, 202–206, 210–213, 220–226,
258–260, 302–305, 325–327, 337–339. There are many pairs of mitzvot that appear in the biblical order and several larger groups in which
the order of only one or two precepts is changed.

8. Such as positive commandments 210–215: to honor parents; to
fear them; to procreate; to marry in law; to free the bridegroom from
public service; to circumcise a son.

the *Sefer HaMitzvot* among the laws of the priesthood,[9] but in *Mishneh Torah* it appears among the laws of prayer.[10]

A. Hilewitz[11] classifies the list on a sevenfold base[12] and describes the difference between the *Sefer HaMitzvot* and *Mishneh Torah* in the relationship of subject and object. The mitzvot in *Mishneh Torah* are arranged in conformity with subjects, while in the *Sefer HaMitzvot* they are in accordance with the objects. Thus, in the example of the priestly benedictions, the subject of the benediction is prayer and blessing, while the object of the precept—the one upon whom it devolves—is the priest.

In this way Hilewitz succeeds in analyzing the enumeration of the *Sefer HaMitzvot* and showing the internal relationship between the individual precept and the wider group of precepts with which it is joined. Apart from offering a solution to the problem of the individual mitzvah and its group, he does not show the similarity in structure that in fact exists between this list and that of *Mishneh Torah*.

Bernhard Ziemlich in his article "Plan und Anlage des Mischne Thora"[13] divides the fourteen books of the *Mishneh Torah* as follows;[14]

9. Positive commandment 26.
10. Chapter 14.
11. In *Sinai* 19: 258–267.
12. (a) The sanctity of the name of heaven, positive commandment 1–19. Prohibition 1–66.

     (b) The sanctity of the Temple, positive commandment 20–91. prohibition 67–171.

     (c) Activity leading to purity, positive commandment 92–152. prohibition 172–231.

     (d) Sanctity of the seasons, positive commandment 153–171.

     (e) Social institutions, positive commandment 172–192.

     (f) Human relationships, positive commandment 193–223. prohibition 232–272.

     (g) Activities of the judiciary, positive commandment 224–248. prohibition 273–365.
13. In Moses ben Maimon, *Schriften Herausgegeben von der Ges-*

BETWEEN MAN AND GOD
Practical Halachah
1. Madda
2. Ahavah
3. Zemanim
4. Nashim
5. Kedushah
6. Haffla'ah

Theoretical Halachah
7. Zeraim
8. Avodah
9. Korbonot
10. Taharah

BETWEEN MAN AND MAN
Practical Halachah
11. Nezikin
12. Kinyan
13. Mishpatim

Theoretical Halachah
14. Shofetim

The books are numbered as they appear in *Mishneh Torah*, so this division is seen to be a completely natural one. On the basis of this division we are able to offer a solution to the problem of the relationship between the two works. For, if we insert the relevant precepts from the *Sefer HaMitzvot* opposite the books of *Mishneh Torah*, the following picture appears:

Apart from the first two books, there is seemingly no parallelism between the groups in *Mishneh Torah* and those in the *Sefer HaMitzvot*. One thing, however, is clear, that the groups in the *Sefer HaMitzvot* certainly parallel the groups in *Mishneh Torah*. The difference in order presents no problem and is easily comprehended as follows.

Because *Mishneh Torah* is intended to be a *practical guide*, clear distinction must be made between the practical and theoretical Halachah. But this division is not a

---

    14. Ibid., p. 278.

Position in Mishneh Torah	Book	Positive Commandments	Position in Sefer HaMitzvot
First	Madda	1–11	First
Second	Ahavah	12–19	Second
Third	Zemanim	153–171	Ninth
Fourth	Nashim	212–223	Eleventh
Fifth	Kedushah	146–152	Eighth
Sixth	Haffla'ah	114–118	Sixth
Seventh	Zeraim	119–145	Seventh
Eighth	Avodah	20–51	Third
Ninth	Korbonoth	52–95	Fourth
Tenth	Taharah	96–113	Fifth
Eleventh	Nezikin		
Twelfth	Kinyan	232–248	Twelfth
Thirteenth	Mishpatim		
Fourteenth	Shofetim	173–211 224–231	Tenth

natural one insofar as the subjects dealt with are concerned. Avodah, Korbonoth, and Taharah, which follow each other in both works, should logically follow Ahavah in *Mishneh Torah;* that they do not is due to their theoretical nature in the time of Maimonides. Haffla'ah is the natural conclusion of this section and is logically followed by Zeraim, dealing with the sanctity of the land as opposed to the sanctity of the Temple. Kedushah (number 8 in the *Sefer HaMitzvot*) is the link between the holy and the ordinary, since some of its laws (e.g., Shechitah) apply to the Temple and some to ordinary life. Then follows (in the *Sefer HaMitzvot*) Sabbaths and festivals, which are independent of the Temple. All of these sections are "between man and God."

"Between man and man" commences (in the *Sefer HaMitzvot*) with the judiciary, as logic dictates, but since the judiciary in postexilic times is in the realm of theoretical Halachah only, the other three books of practical Halachah appear first in *Mishneh Torah*.

In other words, the TaRYaG list of the *Sefer HaMitzvot* arranges the precepts in the groups needed for the books of *Mishneh Torah* and arranges these groups in the simple natural order fitting to them. When Maimonides came to arrange *Mishneh Torah* he realized that it would be imprudent and marring to mix the practical with the theoretical Halachot, and he therefore altered the order of the groups in *Sefer HaMitzvot*. The integral nature of the two works is, however, clearly demonstrated, as is the manner in which the *Sefer HaMitzvot* acts as a blueprint for *Mishneh Torah*.

II

There remain two minor points worthy of mention in discussing the relationship between the two works.

In the nineteenth chapter of Hilchot Sanhedrin, Maimonides lists the 163 prohibitions that carry corporal punishment, but he does not list them in the order of the prohibitions in the *Sefer HaMitzvot*.[15] In this chapter, where Maimonides also lists the other types of prohibitions, it is important to note that he enumerates them on the basis of punishments, in similar manner to the list of the author of the *Halachot Gedolot* and the Mishnah.[16]

The second point concerns the fact that there are many instances where Maimonides appears to contradict

---

15. On this fact see *Zohar Harakiah*, end of Root Nine, and Kalenberg, sec. of Kellalim, rule 4.

16. Cf. chap. 4 n. 55.

statements made in the *Sefer HaMitzvot* by what he writes in *Mishneh Torah*.[17] Many of these instances are, however, due to faulty texts of the *Sefer HaMitzvot,* as Heller clearly proves.[18] In other cases Maimonides indeed changed his mind. In any event, neither the *Sefer HaMitzvot* nor the commentary to the Mishnah that preceded it can be, or are, considered for practical halachic purposes when they contradict *Mishneh Torah.*

There remains a further list of TaRYaG, written by Maimonides, that requires attention. This is the list that appears in the third part of the *Guide to the Perplexed.*[19]

In this list the headings of the fourteen classes into which the laws are subdivided are those used in *Mishneh Torah,* although in the case of five of them it is the subtitles of *Mishneh Torah* that are used.[20] The order of the sections differs materially from those in *Mishneh Torah;* thus, Ahavah appears as the ninth section instead of second, while Kinyan and Mishpatim appear seventh in place of twelfth and thirteenth respectively.

The reason for this difference is that Maimonides' criterion in classifying the precepts in order to expound their reason (it is for this reason and purpose that the list appears in the *Guide*) is, as stated by him in a previous chapter,[21] that all the precepts may be divided under three headings, namely "opinions, morals, and social conduct" and "these three principles suffice for assigning a reason

---

17. See Heller, preface, p. 14; Kalenberg, p. 12b and n. 3, and ibid., paragraph nos. 31, 56, 79, 90, 162.

18. Preface, p. 13.

19. Chapters 35 to 49.

20. *Yesodei HaTorah,* Avodah Zarah, Deot, Ma'achalot Assurot, and Isuurei Biah.

21. Chapter 31.

for every one of the divine commandments." In discussing the mitzvot in the light of this criterion, it is to be expected that their halachic order should be discarded.

In addition to the general, ethical, and explanatory remarks that are liberally scattered throughout the list of precepts,[22] Maimonides includes the following eight points[23] where relevant in connection with each mitzvah.[24]

1. The number of the precept and whether it is a positive commandment or a prohibition. In certain precepts[25] he replaces the usual formula, "Precept so and so we are commanded that . . ." with "Precept so and so the Torah . . ."

2. The exact definition of the precept. In spite of his intention to be brief and exact, Maimonides does not hesitate to explain at length exactly what he means when he feels that conciseness might lead to error.

3. The source of the precept in the Bible. The biblical verses are quoted for each precept, but it is not necessarily the literal verse. It is the verse from which the Oral Law deduces the mitzvah.

   In a responsum,[26] R. Abraham, the son of Maimonides, replying to one who had questioned a biblical source in the *Sefer HaMitzvot,* says, "The first

---

22. Such as prohibition 290, where he gives his views on circumstantial evidence.

23. The author of the Chinuch (see chap. 8) embraces these same points in a threefold treatment of the mitzvah and adds as a fourth point the reason for the precept.

24. Cf. his remarks at the end of Root Fourteen.

25. Positive commandments 108, 114, 115, 117, 145, 243, 244, 245, and 248.

26. Quoted by J. L. Moinester, *Seder HaMitzvot* (New York, 1945), p. 70.

answer, and it is a fundamental issue in our religion, by which we, the congregation of the Rabbinites, are separated from the Karaites, is that we do not rely on the simple (or literal) rendering of the verse but on that which the verse, together with the tradition, teaches."[27]

On two occasions[28] Maimonides includes a precept that is not stated in the Torah. He includes them because the Rabbis declared them to be "of the body of the Torah."[29]

4. Proof from the Talmud and traditional sources. This is necessary because there are many verses that, as they stand, cannot be recognized as precepts without further investigation. In any case it is only possible to invest a biblical verse with preceptive force if the Oral Law indeed holds it to be so, as Maimonides himself says,[30] "Logic would indeed require it to be one mitzvah, but our Sages consider it to be two precepts."

5. He states which other laws, deduced from the same verse, are not separately enumerated[31] in the TaR-YaG list.

6. The punishment for transgression or neglect is stated.

7. He states which persons are free from the particular precept.

---

27. Cf. also Maimonides' remark on the Karaites in positive commandment 153.
28. Prohibitions 135, 336. See also chap. 2 n. 41.
29. See Root Two.
30. Positive commandment 82.
31. Cf. the remarks in the previous chapter on Root Nine.

8. Each mitzvah concludes with a brief reference as to where in the Talmud the subject is comprehensively treated.

At the end of the list of positive commandments, Maimonides makes several important remarks. He summarizes those precepts that apply to the community as a whole and those that apply only to particular individuals, and also those that are dependent upon times and circumstances. He enumerates sixty commandments that, if one be "living in conditions similar to those prevailing for most men; that is to say, that he be dwelling in a house, and in a community, eating such foods as are common to man—namely, bread and meat—dealing with people, taking a wife, and bringing forth children,"[32] fall upon him for fulfillment, in all times and wherever he may live.

---

32. The translation is Chavell's. The 60 precepts are, following the order of the *Sefer HaMitzvot:* nos. 1–15, 18, 19, 26, 32, 54, 73, 94, 143, 146, 147, 149, 150, 152, 154–162, 168–170, 172, 175, 184, 195, 197, 206–215. Women are free from 14 of these, namely, 10, 11, 12, 13, 14, 18, 26, 161, 168, 169, 170, 212, 214, 215. About 200 of the prohibitions apply today. They are enumerated by Chavell, p. 387 n. 1. Cf. also the remarks of the author of the Chinuch in his letter (printed in most editions before the introduction) in this connection. He arrives at a total of 369 precepts and prohibitions that, according to circumstances, are presently obligatory.

8

The Contribution of the Tosafists

The methods of Torah study, differing from those that marked the Geonic period in Babylon and that the Tosafists adopted in Europe,[1] were hardly conducive to the compilation of works enumerating the precepts. Nevertheless, three of the greatest Tosafists devoted themselves to works of this type.

The first was the renowned pupil of R. Yaacob Tam (the master and inspiration of all Tosafists), R. Eliezer of Metz, author of the Sefer Yeraim.

The second was Moses of Coucy, pupil of R. Judah Sir Leon, who reestablished the Beth Hamidrash in Paris in 1198 after the expulsion of the Jews from the city by Phillip in 1182 had forced its doors to close.[2]

---

1. See the penetrating remarks of M. Reich in the *Sinai Jubilee Volume* (Jerusalem, 1958), pp. 356–358.
2. R. Judah himself was a pupil of R. Isaac, nephew of R. Tam.

The third was Isaac of Corbeil,[3] pupil of MaHaRam of Rothenburg, the illustrious leader of troubled Franco-German Jewry during the second half of the thirteenth century.

The motive behind the compilation of each of these works was different.

Eliezer of Metz represents in some measure a revolt against the excessive preoccupation of the Tosafists with Pilpul at the expense of the study of practical Halachah, and he strives for balance and perspective in Torah study. He declares in his preface to the Yeraim:

> For those poor in Torah, labor amongst the dialectic problems of the Talmud and its paths, while as far as the bases of the mitzvot are concerned, they set not their heart to that which the Creator enjoined or to how they may fulfill His statutes and ordinances.

He himself was fully immersed in the method of the Tosafists, but his work is directed to a thorough understanding of the practical Halachah that flows from the precepts. He always quotes the talmudic sources and paves the way to practice by showing what the Halachah is in a given instance. Only the final decisions of his teachers and contemporaries are quoted.

Moses of Coucy was impelled by the opposite extreme. Not the preoccupation with a branch of Torah study, but the open assimilation and indifference to religious practice, rampant in Spanish Jewry, caused him to compile his work.

Isaac of Corbeil felt the need for an authoritative, moral, and halachic presentation of the precepts that could

---

3. Known also as Isaac Ba'al HaChotem, see Urbach, p. 467 and n. 1.

be used beneficially by scholar and layman alike. He alone of the three succeeded to any extent in offering an enumeration and discussion of the precepts free from the dialectic of the Tosafists.

A further point of difference between the works lies in the fact that, while Moses of Coucy is saturated with Maimonides' *Mishneh Torah* and Isaac of Corbeil modeled his work on that of Moses of Coucy,[4] Eliezer of Metz seems to know nothing of Maimonides, and he bases his list on that of the author of the *Halachot Gedolot* and the opinions of the Franco-German schools.

THE SEFER YERAIM[5]

We have already pointed out the reason for the compilation of this work. The work is unique as far as Jewish literature of the period is concerned, since it underwent considerable change in form at the hands of a later editor[6] and was long known only in its edited form.

Originally the precepts were divided into 464 paragraphs (some containing more than one mitzvah) grouped in seven sections called Amudim, pillars.[7] The original sections were:

1. Laws relating to forbidden marriages.
2. Laws relating to food.

4. In his preface he states, "Whoever does not understand the explanation offered should consult the *Sefer Hamitzvot* of R. Moses of Coucy."

5. Literally, "Those Who Fear." So called, as the author states in his preface, "For from it they will learn to fear the Lord." Urbach, p. 139, places the date of its compilation between 1171 and 1179.

6. See Shem HaGedolim, no. 197, and Jellineck, Kontres TaRYaG, no. 67.

7. Probably with Proverbs 9:1 in mind.

3. Laws relating to that from which benefit is forbidden.
4. Financial matters.
5. Matters forbidden between man and God and between man and man that do not involve theft or financial benefit.
6. Matters forbidden that render one sinful in the eyes of God but not in the sight of man.
7. Matters forbidden that render one sinful in the sight of heaven but are independent of speech.

These were changed about a hundred years after the work had been written by Benjamin son of Abraham the physician,[8] who divided the precepts into 417 paragraphs and grouped them under twelve pillars, to which he gave entirely new names.[9] The names that Benjamin gave to the pillars show that he was undoubtedly influenced by *Mishneh Torah*.

The original plan and order of the Yeraim was seen by Azulai in manuscript form in the Royal library of Paris. It was published as the Yeraim Hashalem ("Complete Yeraim") by A. A. Schiff of Minsk during the years of 1894–1904.

In following the author of the *Halachot Gedolot*, rabbinic precepts[10] are included. The majority of precepts commence with the formula "The Holy One, Blessed be He, commanded" or "The Holy One, Blessed be He, enjoined at Sinai," but there are occasions when he commences a precept with a verse from the prophets.[11] In one

8. His edition of the Yeraim was first published in Venice in 1565.
9. (1) Fear of God; (2) idolatry; (3) seasons; (4) food; (5) seeds; (6) sexual relationships; (7) civil law; (8) kings (judiciary); (9) purity; (10) vows; (11) the Temple, its priests, and vessels; (12) sacrifices.
10. For example, paras. 10 and 128.
11. Paragraphs 1, 12, 18, etc.

instance,[12] he copies a precept found in the *Halachot Gedolot* but commences with the words: "It is fitting for a person." He concludes the paragraph with the remark that he finds no basis for this precept in the Torah. Several precepts commence with "And thou shalt fear God,"[13] while some have a more prosaic beginning.[14]

Numerous precepts are dealt with at great length,[15] and entire sections of the Talmud are quoted verbatim in discussing them. In particular, in the precept concerning phylacteries,[16] the talmudic discussion concerning every detail of their manufacture, including even the type of ink that is to be used, is quoted, while the precept concerning the sabbath[17] contains an analysis of all the classes of prohibited work.

The pillars conclude with the author's statement of the number of precepts in each pillar, and a Gematria (i.e., a Hebrew word giving the numerical equivalent) is found in an appropriate verse.

The work is considered one of the most important halachic productions of the period.

THE SEFER MITZVOT GADOL

Moses of Coucy[18] was also known, by virtue of the extensive preaching to "the exiles of Israel" undertaken during

---

12. Paragraph 22.

13. Paragraphs 9, 117, 118, 120.

14. "May our Creator, who has given Torah in our midst and has enjoined His fear upon us, be Blessed," no. 298. "To He who formed you give praise and thanks and admit that the earth is His," no. 345.

15. 13, 15, 16, 17, 18, 19, 24, 102, 105, 113, 123, 124, 183, 192, 270, 272, 311, 325, 352.

16. Number 16.

17. Number 102.

18. 1200?–1260. He was a grandson of R. Hayyim HaCohen, the pupil of R. Yaacob Tam, and his reverence for his grandfather is shown

his travels, as Moses the Preacher.[19] Indeed, much of his fame during the thirteenth century rested upon his preaching ability, which was responsible for a mass return to Judaism in the Spanish Peninsula. His itinerant preaching led directly to the compilation and nature of his famous work the Sefer Mitzvot Gadol. Such was his prestige that he, together with three other scholars, was chosen to represent the Jewish community at the disputes concerning the Talmud, which took place in Paris in the years 1240 and 1242.

However, he took no part at all in the controversy that had previously (in 1232) broken out in Provence and that later spread to Spain, concerning Maimonides' works. On the contrary, his unbounded admiration for Maimonides, expressed in his preface to the prohibitions, where he says, "There arose a great man, our teacher Moses, son of Maimon of Cordova, who wrote on the entire Torah a delightful and praiseworthy work that enlightened the eyes of all Israel. And in all wisdoms he was wondrous, and there has not been his like in these latter generations," and his continual reliance on Maimonides' opinion,[20] except where the Tosafists differ from him, must have done much to establish Maimonides' authority among the Franco-German schools.

The Sefer Mitzvot Gadol contains two extremely interesting prefaces, one for the prohibitions, which is

by the title "high priest," which he ascribes to him (positive commandment 231). His teacher, Judah Sir Leon, is quoted throughout the work. See Hones, Toldot Haposkim (New York, 1946), pp. 393–395. E. E. Urbach, *The Tosafists* (Jerusalem, 1955), pp. 384 ff.

19. Not to be confused, as some scholars have done, with Moses the Preacher of Narbonne. See Urbach, p. 385 n. 6.

20. He very often quotes Maimonides word for word. Solomon Luria responsum 35 says, "Sefer Mitzvot Gadol is completely founded on Maimonides' work."

the first part of the work, the other to the positive commandments.

The first preface, with its brief outline of the chain of tradition and mention of the works of his predecessors, seems to have been inspired by the prefaces of Maimonides to his works. However, the difference between the two is immediately apparent. The preface to Sefer Mitzvot Gadol is written with the intention of persuading the general, unlearned public. The first half of it is devoted to illustrations that show the need for the Oral Law to explain biblical contradictions, inconsistencies, and obscurities. This section concludes with a quotation from the Pirkei D'Reb Eliezer, which explains the reason for the oral transmission of tradition. The quotation reads:

Because the Holy One, Blessed be He, saw that the peoples of the world would copy the twenty-four books that are contained in the Pentateuch, Prophets, and Writings, and distort their meaning into evil and free-thinking, He gave oral signs to Moses. And heaven did not agree to write them down until after the establishment of the faiths of Edom (Christianity) and Ishmael (Mohammedanism) lest the non-Jews copy them and distort them as they have done with the Written Law. In the world to come the Holy One, Blessed be He, will ask, "Who are my children?" The children of Israel will bring a Sefer Torah and the peoples will also bring a Sefer Torah. These will claim to be His children and these will claim to be His children. And the Holy One, Blessed be He, will ask, "Who has the signs that I gave orally to Moses at Sinai?" And none will know them but Israel.

Quoted in this preface, the passage fully illustrates the concern felt by the author both at the ignorance of the Oral Law and the drift toward Christianity that he found among the Jewish community in Spain. This latter fear is emphasized by him in the concluding remarks of the second preface, where he says:

And after the death of Moses our teacher there arose prophets in Israel who spoke in riddles and parables and concealed words, and because of this the non-Jews claim that the prophets foretold their new lore.

The work, therefore, was written with an important object in mind. Its conception arose from the dire religious plight in which he found the Peninsula Jewish communities. Sefer Mitzvot Gadol contains, in fact, a mine of historical information and data on the Jewish communities of the period. Intermarriage was rampant,[21] they did not observe the precepts of phylacteries, fringes, or mezuzah,[22] while their moral and ethical relationship with the non-Jewish community was one that entitled them to be called "a people of swindlers and thieves."[23]

Although during the course of his travels R. Moses had been urged to compile a short explanatory work on the precepts in order to facilitate the repentance of the

---

21. See prohibition 112, where he says, "And I preached extensively (on intermarriage) among the exiles of Jerusalem who are in Spain, and they divorced many foreign women, Christians and Mohammedans, in the year 1236, praise be to God."

22. Positive commandment 3, where he says that after his visit in the year 1236, "they performed great penances and thousands and tens of thousands accepted upon themselves the mitzvot of phylacteries, fringes, and mezuzah."

23. Prohibition 2, end. positive commandment 73. Cf. also Yeraim 260 in this connection.

communities concerned,[24] he hesitated before doing so. It was only because:

> at the beginning of the sixth millenium (after 1240) that I received a vision in a dream, which said, "Arise and make a Sefer Torah of two parts." And I thought deeply about the vision, and behold, the two parts consist of the positive precepts and the prohibitions that I, Moses, son of Jacob, set myself to compile the two works.

The work is primarily intended to enumerate TaRYaG while showing briefly and as simply as possible both their organic relationship with the Oral Law and how, in consequence of this relationship, they are to be fulfilled in practice.

The order of the two lists is a parallel one, the groupings of the prohibitions being followed by the same groupings and the same order in the list of positive commandments. He follows the order of the books of *Mishneh Torah*,[25] with the exception that all the precepts pertaining to practical Halachah precede those that are today only theoretical.[26] The section on the positive commandments is followed by treatment of several rabbinic ordinances,[27] and many more are treated in the body of the work.[28] The fullest consideration is given to the texts of

---

24. End of preface and positive commandment 3.

25. See chap. 7.

26. He offers a spirited defense in the second preface of study of those sections of Torah that are today only theoretical.

27. Erubin, Avel, Tisha B'av, Megillah, Chanukkah.

28. In conformity with his statement in the preface that "as they study this work, in each precept they will see how the Rabbis made a fence around the Torah."

the Oral Law, its codifiers and its commentaries, and numerous authorities are quoted. In spite of his attempt at
brevity, Tosafist that he was, he is unable to avoid many
dialectic excursions into the talmudic field.[29]

Aggadah plays almost as much a part in the work as
does Halachah, while his own sermons and exhortations
are liberally scattered throughout. This fact led to the
widespread popularity of the work. Halachists treated it as
an authoritative halachic code, and they compiled numerous commentaries to it.[30] The references to the codes,
which appear on each page of the Talmud, refer one to the
works of Maimonides, Tur, and Sefer Mitzvot Gadol, which
fact abundantly illustrates the esteem in which the work
was, and is yet, held.

Such was the popularity of Sefer Mitzvot Gadol that
shortened forms of it,[31] including the author's own shortened version,[32] did not succeed in reducing the popularity
and demand for the original.

---

29. It has been suggested that the reason for the compilation of the
work is to be found in the fact of the burning of the Talmud and
prohibition of its study in France by Ludwig the Ninth. This may well
account for the abundance of talmudic quotation found in the work,
which is to be considered in the light of bringing the banned Talmud to
the masses. However, his remarks quoted above, from the preface to
the work, contain no hint of this being the cause of his work. On the
contrary, he stresses the fact *that he does not quote the actual texts of
the Talmud* and that his original intention was to list the precepts *for his
personal benefit*—to commit them to memory for use in his sermons
while traveling among the communities of Israel.

30. Among the most famous of these are Obadia Bertinoro, Eliahu
Mizrachi, Joseph Colon, Solomon Luria, and Isaac Stern.

31. See Jellineck, nos. 120 and 130.

32. See Shem Hagedolim, p. 101, no. 178. There is, however, genuine doubt as to whether the author himself in fact shortened his larger
work. See the note to "Kitzur Sefer Mitzvot Gadol" (Warsaw, 1894), p.
8, and also the note of Menachem Zion to the Shem Hagedolim, loc. cit.

The enumeration differs, but not greatly, in both parts, from the enumeration of Maimonides.[33]

R. Moses mentions in his preface that before setting out on his travels he memorized TaRYaG, together with the main points that each mitzvah involved. This might possibly be the origin of the custom, stressed by many,[34] of reciting TaRYaG weekly in order to learn the list by heart. Urbach mentions[35] that the scholars of France, who were greatly influenced by the piety of Isaac of Corbeil, copied the latter's list of precepts into their prayer books for daily recital, in place of the Book of Psalms and other additional prayers. In fact the author sent copies far and wide with the intention and hope of popularizing the list of precepts.[36] He

33. He removes Maimonides' positive commandments 142, 193, and 198, and substitutes: (1) To justify the divine judgment (Deuteronomy 8:5. *Berakhot* 60. *Eruvin* 40a). *Halachot Gedolot* also includes this precept, as does Sefer Mitzvot Kattan (no. 5). But see *Zohar Harakiah* positive commandment n. 15. (2) To reckon the seasons (Deuteronomy 4:6. *Shabbat* 75a). Maimonides in Root Two objects to *Halachot Gedolot*'s inclusion of this precept. (3) To keep far from falsehood (Exodus 23:7. *Shevi'it* 31a). *Zohar Harakiah* also includes this precept, n. 59 to positive commandments. He removes the following prohibitions from Maimonides' list: nos. 14, 67, 71, 78, 95, 140, 151, 152, 165, 177, 178, 199, 266, 278, 283, 291. Nachmanides agrees with Sefer Mitzvot Gadol concerning 71, 95, 177, 178, and 199, while Sefer Mitzvot Gadol expresses doubt concerning 199 (Sefer Mitzvot Gadol, 76); 291 (Sefer Mitzvot Gadol, 264). On 152 and 151, see Mitzvot Hashem, paras. 608–610. One precept, "Not to depart from the Torah" (included also by Yeraim no. 28, and Sefer Mitzvot Kattan no. 15), he included as the result of a dream (preface).

34. Especially by Shabbattai HaCohen (SHaCH) in the preface to his Poel Tzedeck, reprinted together with Pe'er Hamitzvot (New York, 1948).

35. Page 449.

36. See preface to Sefer Mitzvot Kattan and Shem Hagedolim, pt. 2, no. 62. This fact is responsible for the large number of manuscript copies of Sefer Mitzvot Kattan that have survived and that have

even advocates in his preface that the synagogue authorities pay from public funds for copies to be made and distributed.

THE SEFER MITZVOT KATTAN[37]

This work is distinctive among the three in that it treats only of those precepts obligatory after the destruction of the Temple. For this reason the original title of the work, Shiv'a Amudei Olam" ("The Seven Pillars of the World," paralleling the Seven Days of the Week), was relegated to obscurity and the work is best known as Amudei HaGolah ("The Pillars of the Exile").

The precepts are divided into seven lists, one for recital on each day,[38] while in addition to this regular recital of the plain list, study of the explanation of "two or three precepts," contained in the body of the work is urged. The author stresses this study since "the ignorant

---

marginal notes appended to them. Cf. the remarks of Assaf, Be'ohalei Yaacob, p. 13.

37. Some authorities read Katzar, Short, since Sefer Mitzvot Kattan is almost a shortened version of Sefer Mitzvot Gadol.

38. The author says in the preface, "And I was afraid that many would not know the explanation of the precepts that are obligatory upon us, so I wrote those precepts applicable today in seven pillars, for the seven days of the week. And I urge each one to read one pillar every day so that it will be well with him. And when he reads them and thinks of their performance, the Holy One, Blessed be He, considers him worthy as if he had performed them." According to the preface of R. Mordechai b. Nathan (pupil of Maharam of Rothenburg) printed in the Constantinople edition of the Sefer Mitzvot Kattan (reprinted in Amudei Hagolah, edited with commandments and critical notes by I. I. Shapiro ([Jerusalem, 1959], pt. 1, p. 15), the author originally only wrote a simple list, each section of which could have been reasonably recited daily. Later, pressed by his contemporaries, he added explanations to the mitzvot.

cannot be pious,"[39] and it sometimes happens that one intends to perform a mitzvah and through ignorance commits a transgression.

The seven pillars are peculiar to the author.[40] They are:

1. Precepts dependent upon the heart (including eyes and ears).
2. Precepts dependent upon the body and time.
3. Precepts dependent upon the tongue and time.
4. Precepts dependent upon the hands (also laws of marriage).
5. Precepts dependent upon eating (also civil matters).
6. Precepts dependent upon money.
7. Precepts connected with Sabbath (festivals and circumcision are included under this pillar).

The Seven Pillars contain 294 sections and include more than 60 precepts listed by Maimonides[41] as obligatory today. This is because the author, in conformity with his intention of embracing all of the practical precepts in his work, includes many rabbinic ordinances[42] and also certain additional biblical precepts that do not appear in Maimonides' list.[43]

---

39. *Ethics of the Fathers*, chap. 2.

40. They are doubtless the origin for the pattern of the Cheradim, by Eliezer Azkari, while the original idea of the Seven Pillars probably stems from the Yeraim.

41. See note at the end of chap. 7.

42. Such as the duty to mourn the destruction of the Temple, no. 96. Also 97, 98, 99, 100, 101, 148, 149, 150, 181, 192, 278, 279, etc.

43. A similar work embracing those precepts obligatory nowadays was compiled by Israel Meir Hacohen, the "Chafetz Chayyim," also called "Sefer Hamitzvot Hakatzar." It contains 77 positive commandments and 194 prohibitions.

The sections outline briefly the practical laws and conditions governing each precept dealt with, and the treatment never becomes obscure.

Sefer Mitzvot Kattan includes as biblical many ethical precepts that do not appear in other TaRYaG lists,[44] and several that are included by the author of the *Halachot Gedolot.*[45] He does not, however, appear to have enumerated the precepts by means of any particular system,[46] and he includes precepts mentioned by *Halachot Gedolot,*[47] Saadya Gaon,[48] Nachmanides,[49] Sefer Mitzvot Gadol,[50] and Duran.[51] The work has a definite ethical coloring, and aggadic sayings and parables are frequent. In one instance[52] he mentions the decorum of the church as an example worthy of being followed by synagogue worshipers.

Notes by Rabbenu Peretz the Tosafist, pupil of the author, appear in every edition of the Sefer Mitzvot Kattan except the first.[53] A shortened version of the work has also appeared.[54]

---

44. Number 9, to love reproof; no. 14, not to be self-righteous; no. 21, not to feel bad when giving charity; no. 22, not to be proud; no. 24, not to harbor evil thoughts.

45. Number 47, to visit the sick; no. 49, to act within the letter of the law; no. 5, to justify the lot meted out by God (Sefer Mitzvot Gadol also, no. 17); no. 46, to act with kindliness.

46. Thus nos. 37–43 enumerate seven separate precepts in connection with the destruction of idolatry.

47. In addition to those mentioned in n. 45, nos. 106, 111, 198, 224, and 239.

48. 38, 52, and 158.

49. Number 10.

50. Numbers 15, 17, and 226.

51. Numbers 28 and 288.

52. Number 11. Cf. also "Sefer Charedim," chap. 1, sec. 19, end.

53. See Jellineck, no. 41. It must, however, be noted that these notes contain many additions by other scholars.

54. Ibid., no. 131.

9

Later Authors

We have seen that during its long history the TaRYaG tradition was put to varying and different uses. The author of the *Halachot Gedolot* places TaRYaG at the beginning of his work in order to counteract Karaite rejection of the rabbinic tradition, and it passed into the liturgy for similar reasons. Chefez, followed by Maimonides, erects the moral, philosophical, and practical world of Judaism around it, while the illustration of the organic relationship between the Written and Oral Laws is centered upon it.

The attempt to restore drifting Peninsula Jewry to halachic Judaism is undertaken by its means, while the popularity of the tradition is the vehicle used to restore balance and the study of fundamentals among Franco-German Jewry.

However, in spite of the diverse use to which it had already been put, the tradition had by no means lost its force by the thirteenth century. Indeed, it continued to reflect phases of Jewish life and thought for centuries. It became both a maid of all work and a faithful mirror of historical conditions and intellectual change.

It is impossible to treat comprehensively the numerous TaRYaG works that have appeared since the thirteenth century. In this concluding chapter, however, an attempt is made to treat briefly five works, each of which aspired to play an important part in the ignorant, troubled, or creative age of the author. In addition to this reason, they have been chosen because they are still today both authoritative and popular.

While the early half of thirteenth-century Spain was dominated by the halachic TaRYaG of Moses of Coucy, the latter part of the century, and indeed subsequent centuries, were captivated by the moral and ethical TaRYaG of Aaron of Barcelona. The low ebb of scholarship found by Peninsula exiles in North Africa once again brings forth a halachic TaRYaG of excellence, while, a century later, the flowering of mysticism in Safed gives birth to the mystical TaRYaG of Isaiah Horowitz.

The seventeenth-century Shabbataian calamity gives rise to the zealous, faith-inspiring TaRYaG of Moses Hagiz, while the nineteenth-century apostate Moses Margoliouth in England can ridicule the religion of his fathers in no better manner than by compiling a treatise on TaRYaG.

Sefer Hachinuch (The Educator)

The purpose of the work is declared by the author, both in the preface and in the additional remarks to Leviticus, to have been to introduce his son, as well as youngsters of his son's age, to an understanding of the precepts. Also, "to capture their thoughts with clean and important considerations, before their minds become filled with thoughts of laughter and nonsense."

His concluding words to the Book of Leviticus are, "and behold I again wish to remind you, as I have already apologized many times, concerning the reasons for the precepts that my heart urged me to pen, that my intention has only been to educate the young men and to show them that the precepts enshrine great purposes that are open for all to see, as they are able to grasp even in their early years. I therefore called this work the Educator. The depths of wisdom and great purposes of the mitzvot they will, if they merit it, perceive when they are older."[1] That the work was intended as an introduction to further self-study is evident from expressions such as "inquire into it," "and if you will merit, you will understand," and "seek it there," in which the work abounds.[2]

The author of this famous work was Aaron of Barcelona, a Levite.[3] The Hebrew mnemonic of his name, ReAH, [R(Rabbi) eA(Aaron) H(Halevi)], led to his being confused with Aaron Halevi, the pupil of Nachmanides and

---

1. The son of the author is mentioned twenty-one times in the work, precepts 20, 95, 126, 164, 243, 285, 288, 316, 321, 325, 326, 343, 345, 390, 397, 424, 428, 465, 537, 549, and 554. In spite of this, the work is obviously directed also to the scholar. The author's halachic independence is abundantly demonstrated throughout, e.g., precept 27, 147, etc. In precepts 163 and 573, he declares categorically that Maimonides is in error.

2. In precept 330 he says, "And I have completed this my task in having posed the question for you."

3. In the preface he calls himself "A Jew, a Levite from Barcelona." The first edition of the work (Venice, 1523) has "The Sefer Hachinuch of R. Aaron of Blessed memory," on the frontispiece.

well-known author of several halachic works. Azulai[4] was
the first to point out the error of ascribing the Chinuch to
this scholar. In fact, the author seems to have been Aaron
Halevi, pupil of Adereth,[5] of whom little is known.

The Chinuch is based upon the TaRYaG works of
Maimonides and Nachmanides.[6] In spite, however, of
strict[7] adherence to Maimonides' list, he does not hesitate
to agree with Nachmanides[8] or to state his own opinion[9] or
even to leave the preference to "the scholar, who may
select the correct opinion for himself."[10] But he does not
allow either his own opinion, or that of Maimonides'
critics, to alter Maimonides' TaRYaG list. In one instance[11]
he says, "It is not entirely acceptable to consider this a
precept. Nevertheless, we will not turn aside from the path
of our teacher in enumerating the precepts."[12]

---

4. Shem Hagedolim, no. 132.

5. On this complicated question see Sapher Hachinuch, edition
with introduction and notes, according to the Venice edition by C. D.
Chavel, 4th ed. (Jerusalem, 1960), pp. 799–806. Chavel places the date
of compilation between 1274 and 1310. See also "Sefer Hazikkaron" of
R. Yom Tob b. Abraham, ed. K. Kahana (Jerusalem, 1956), app. 3, p. 77.
Chones, Told. Hapos. p. 260, c. 2, is mistaken in this matter.

6. His admiration for both of his predecessors knows no bounds.
He says of them (164 and 485), "Their opinions are words of the Living
God," while of Maimonides he says (285), "For he is an angel of the
Lord of Hosts."

7. But see Mitzvot Hashem, para. 103. Chinuch, precept III.

8. Precepts 138, 153, 159, 160, 161, 379, 111, etc.

9. Precepts 147, 98, 163, 285, 298, 314, 320, 550.

10. Precepts 47, 164.

11. Precept 161. Cf. also 156, 169, and 573.

12. This statement seems convincing enough to reject identification of the author with the pupil of Nachmanides, who certainly never
hesitated to reject Maimonides' opinion when he felt it necessary. In
any event, the author quotes "my teachers" side by side with quotations from Nachmanides throughout the work.

Discussion of each precept is divided into four sections:

(1) The identity and definition of the precept, its biblical source and rabbinic interpretation. This section is based primarily upon Maimonides.

(2) The reasons for the mitzvot. It is in this section of the work that the true originality of the author emerges. He draws freely upon both Maimonides and Nachmanides, but whereas the former approaches the reasons for mitzvot from the philosophical standpoint and the latter is based upon the mystical understanding of Torah, the author, while accepting Maimonides' standpoint that each precept has purpose[13] and realizing that indeed the deeper realms of Torah are discoverable by means of the mystical approach, bases his understanding of the precepts on religious, ethical, and social considerations.

For you see that there is in the precepts of the Torah reason; to benefit man's thoughts—to make him upright—to train him, so that all his deeds may be fitting. Their purpose is not, far be it, for the good of the Creator.[14]

He negates Maimonides' attribution of many precepts to a negation of idolatry,[15] but agrees with him in refusing to discuss the reason for all the details of the precepts.[16]

Ethical statements abound throughout the work and form the cornerstone of the religious outlook of the author:

---

13. See precept 117.
14. See precept 545.
15. Precept 92, where he says, "and all this is valueless in my eyes."
16. Precept 104.

"Nothing is as abominable as falsehood."[17]

"The blessing of God is merited by purity of thought."[18]

"The way of the pious is to love peace and rejoice in the happiness of men."[19]

"Rejection is due to an impure soul, not to one's trade."[20]

"One must be kind to animals."[21]

"Acquire the habits of kindness and mercy."[22]

"Evil thoughts are the fathers of impurities, deeds their result."[23]

"He who maltreats his servant, trains himself in arrogance, and as good as testifies that he is not of the seed of Israel, for they are merciful descendants of merciful fathers."[24]

Speculation on a different plane is not absent from the work,[25] but this is accompanied by touching humility.[26] His concern for the poor and the needy[27] and his love for the people of Israel are felt throughout.

17. Precept 74.
18. Precept 269.
19. Precept 529.
20. Precept 88.
21. Precept 596.
22. Precepts 42, 44, and 63.
23. Precept 387.
24. Precept 42.
25. Preface, where he treats why Israel suffers in Exile. Precept 16, precept 416, etc.
26. Introduction, precept 95, etc. In precepts 95, 159, etc., he touches also on the limitations inherent in offering reasons for the precepts.
27. In speaking of the offering of the poor man (precept 124), he says, "And one should glorify the sacrifice of the poor man with all one's strength. Enough that he has poverty, we should not add to it by deriding the description of his sacrifice."

(3) The laws of each precept. The author in this section gives an outline of the essential laws of each precept. He draws with masterly precision the dividing line between the biblical and rabbinic elements of each precept. Although he relies in the main upon *Mishneh Torah*, he quotes copiously from original sources as well as from numerous predecessors and contemporaries.

Many precepts are dealt with at length,[28] and details of practical halachic necessity are not spared. He explains many biblical verses,[29] rabbinic sayings,[30] and incidents[31] and introduces several new halachic principles[32] and interpretations.[33] He also deals at length with anthropomorphisms,[34] stressing that these are used only so that "the listener will understand."[35]

(4) A summary explaining by whom, where, and when the mitzvah is to be fulfilled.

The printed editions of the Chinuch indicate that the author of this work was the first to list the precepts according to their order in the weekly readings of the Torah.[36] An examination of the first edition of the Chinuch, as well as of

---

28. For example, precepts 30, 111, 148, 430, etc.

29. For example, precept 510.

30. For example, precepts 16, 263, 425, 545, etc.

31. Precepts 30 and 496.

32. Precepts 26, 43, 123, etc. In precept 66, he asserts that the institution restricting charity to one-fifth of one's wealth, *Ketubot* 67, during one's lifetime does not apply to lending money to those in need.

33. For example, precepts 69, 91.

34. For example, precept 87.

35. Compare also his remarks on the "shewbread" and sacrifices in general, precept 97, etc.

36. As we have shown above, previous lists enumerate TaRYaG under the positive and prohibitive lists, according to the author's own arrangement, or, as in the case of the Yeraim, arrange the precepts in a manner entirely of their choosing.

early manuscripts, shows this to be mistaken. The Chinuch also enumerated the precepts according to the two accepted lists. His originality lay in the fact that, for pedagogical reasons outlined in his introduction, his lists of positive and prohibitive precepts follow the order in which they appear in the Torah and not a preconceived logical pattern. But the two lists are distinct, the positive precepts in the pericope being listed before the prohibitions.[37]

The first to list the precepts exactly in the order they appear in the Torah, mingling the positive and prohibitive precepts, was Isaiah Horowitz, author of *Shene Luchoth Habrith*, who was followed by Shabbattai Cohen in the latter's Poel Tzedek.[38]

The first edition of the Chinuch in the order in which it appears today was printed in Frankfurt on Oder in 1783,[39] and the editor, in his rearrangement of the work, was doubtless influenced by Shene Luchoth Habrith and Shabbattai Cohen.

Zohar Harakiah (Brightness of the Firmament)

Zohar Harakiah is a halachic work of eminence. Written by Simon b. Zemach Duran[40] after his exile to Algiers— "and the work was completed in Algiers, the city of our

37. It is possible that the Chinuch, printed by Bomberg in 1523, was known by Felix Pratensis and incorporated by him in Bomberg's first rabbinic Bible of 1517, from there to appear in many subsequent rabbinic Bibles.

38. First published Yasnitz, 1720.

39. Other changes also appear in this edition; see Chavel, introduction, pp. XX, no. 4.

40. Born 1361 in Barcelona, died 1444 in Algiers. He left Aragon, where he enjoyed a flourishing medical practice, penniless, owing to the decrees of 1391. He soon came to occupy a prominent position in the North African community. He was related by marriage to Nachmanides' family. See the genealogical table in Jonah b. Abraham of Gerona, A. T. Shrock, p. 19.

sojournings, on the second day of the month Sivan in the year five thousand one hundred and seventy seven"—it is noteworthy in three ways.

First, it is written in the form of a commentary to the Azharah "Shemor Libbi Ma'aneh" of Ibn Gabirol. Strange practice for a halachist of such eminence[41] but, as he himself explains, the reason for this was, "For I see that men of worth are few[42] and none seek after deep works. Therefore I arranged the matter around this Azharah so that people who tremble for the word of the Lord should study it once a year."[43]

Duran criticizes[44] previous commentaries to this Azharah for their having mistakenly interpreted it according to Maimonides' TaRYaG list. Gabirol followed *Halachot Gedolot* and, in the understanding of the Azharah, Duran remains faithful to this fact.

The second factor is that of the author's halachic style, which has almost no parallel in halachic works of the period. In consideration for the intellectual level of his audience, the Hebrew style[45] is simple and flows smoothly. Difficult forms of expression are singularly absent from the work. The most abstruse halachic discussions are, as a result, easily comprehended.

The third and most important feature of the work lies in the actual treatment of the precepts.

Maimonides' and Nachmanides' opinions are treated briefly, and the essential proofs and objections to each are given. Throughout, clarity and decision prevail. Duran

---

41. The comparison with Saadya Gaon is obvious.

42. In the foreword he describes his disgust at the ignorance and gross habits prevalent among the Algiers community.

43. The Azharah was recited on the festival of Shavuot.

44. Notes 11, 12, etc.

45. Aramaisms are almost nonexistent in the work.

does not hesitate to criticize both of his predecessors, and his own proofs, or objections to their opinions, abound. In a halachic sense he is a "Machria" (a decisor) between the two, although he rejects both of their opinions when he feels this warranted. As a result of his penetrating treatment and criticism of their work, he is forced to include twenty-four positive precepts and eighteen prohibitions that appear in neither of their lists in order to complete his TaRYaG list.

Among the most noteworthy of these are the precepts: "to accept proselytes,"[46] "to keep far from falsehood,"[47] and "to repay a creditor."[48]

Shene Luchoth Habrith (SHeLaH)
(The Two Tablets of Stone)

Isaiah Horowitz,[49] famed as a talmudist and moralist, approached TaRYaG not because he was interested in TaRYaG for its own sake; in fact, he follows Maimonides without deviation.[50] He considered his enumeration necessary for the correct fulfillment of the rabbinic injunction[51] "that

---

46. Addition 4.

47. Addition 14.

48. Addition 17.

49. Born in Prague in 1555, he was renowned among communities in Germany for both scholarship and piety. He left Prague in 1621 and went to Jerusalem. Shene Luchoth Habrith was completed two years after his arrival there. He died in 1630.

50. In his introductory remarks he refutes *Sefer Mitzvot HaGadol* at length, adding, "And I in humility have chosen to enumerate TaRYaG according to Maimonides and not to deviate from him in any way; for him did God choose to grace with understanding, knowledge, and discernment, and were all the winds of the world to blow they could not undermine his Roots."

51. *Berakhot* 8a. In those pericopes with no mitzvah of TaRYaG, he treats ethical obligations pegged to particular incidents or verses, e.g., Genesis, chap. 18, where he expatiates on the duty of hospitality. His treatment of the pericopes in this manner is reminiscent of the Sheiltoth.

each man should complete his reading of the weekly pericope with the congregation, twice with the text and once
with the Targum." Insisting that this injunction does not
mean simply to read the text alone but to delve "according
to one's ability" into the precepts contained in the pericope, he arranged the precepts in the order in which they
appear in the Torah and treated them at length.

His discussion of the precepts is divided into three
parts.[52] The first, which he calls "Ner Mitzvah" (The Light of
the Mitzvah), is the simple identification and listing of the
precept. The second is "Torah Or" (Torah is light or The Light
of the Torah), in which reasons for the mitzvot are advanced,
and the third, "Derekh Chayyim Tochachath Mussar" (The
way of life is Moral Instruction), embraces the ethical lessons
and correct habits inherent in the precept.

On Horowitz's arrival in Eretz Yisrael, he became
greatly influenced by the Lurianic school of Kabballah,
and as a result, the second section, Torah Or contains a
great deal of the mystical interpretation of Torah and
Aggadah. But he succeeds, by means of a lucid, clear
Hebrew, in conveying even conceptions of the Kabbalah in
a manner easily comprehended by one to whom mysticism
is not completely strange. In revealing "but a drop of the
ocean" with such deceptive clarity, he succeeds in stimu-
lating the religious thought and poetic feeling of the individual to a marked degree.

Charedim (Those Who Fear)

Little is known of Eliezer Azkari, the author of Charedim, but
the work, first published in Venice in 1959, is a fitting product
of the moral-mystical school of sixteenth-century Safed.

---

52. Based on Proverbs 6:23.

The lengthy preface, which is followed by eight introductory chapters, deals with philosophical and mystical problems, including an exposition of the Sefirot, and constitutes an inspired exhortation to fulfill the precepts. Seven rules are reproduced at length from the work "Shushan Sodot"[53] as necessary bases for the correct and full observance of the mitzvot in daily life.

Based on the verse, "All my bones shall declare, who is like unto Thee, O Lord,"[54] and in accordance with an ancient tradition quoted by the author from Tannaitic sources, the precepts are divided into eight parts, which correspond with the eight limbs whose activity is required for fulfilling precepts.[55] The precept of fringes, which calls to mind all mitzvot,[56] is separately treated.

The work aims to enumerate only those precepts applicable to Jewry in exile,[57] and a great number of rabbinic ordinances are incorporated in the enumeration. Earlier authorities, including Maimonides, Ibn Gabirol, SeMaG, SeMaK, and Rabbenu Jonah of Gerona, are continually quoted.

The second section of the work deals at great length with those precepts dependent for fulfillment upon residence in the Holy Land, and in this section the author shows himself to have been a halachist of caliber; indeed, he was ordained by the renowned Yaacob Berab.[58] The work concludes with seven chapters on repentance.

---

53. This work was seen by Jellineck in manuscript form. K. T., p. 11, no. 58. But see n. 1, ibid. Azkari himself expands the number of rules and conditions to seventeen, while A. Danziger, in his popular code "Chayye Adam," enumerates twenty-five such conditions.

54. Psalms 35:10.

55. Heart, eye, mouth, nose, ear, hand, foot, and the sexual organ.

56. Numbers 15:39.

57. Cf. Sefer Mitzvot Hakatzar.

58. Shem Hagedolim, no. 212.

A shortened version of Charedim was published in Vilna in 1877. It had been prepared by Abraham Danziger, author of popular codes on Jewish law.

Eleh Hamitzvot (These are the mitzvot).

Moses Hagiz[59] is known for the energetic manner in which he attacked and almost succeeded in destroying the creative ability of Moses Chayyim Luzzatto.[60] This unreasonable on-slaught on Luzzatto, pursued over several years and carried on in all the rabbinic centers of Europe, resulted from the fear that Luzzatto's mysticism might have harbored a revival of the cult of Shabbattai Zevi.[61] Hagiz declared himself against undue preoccupation with mysticism and especially the prac-tical mysticism of Isaac Luria, which was for particular indi-viduals only. He was a halachist of renown, and indeed the declared intention of his work on TaRYaG[62] was in the first instance to provide the unlearned with an easily assimilable introduction to the Oral Law and second to illustrate the organic connection between the Oral and Written Laws. He does not, however, succeed in this task.

The premises of the Oral Law are so self-evident to him that he fails to show how the precepts are in fact linked

---

59. Born in Jerusalem in 1671. He left Eretz Yisrael for Italy in 1688 and died in Safed in 1750.

60. See Ginzberg, Iggerot Ramchal (Dvir, 1937), pt. 1 introduction, at length.

61. In precept 613 he refers to the destructive cult of Sabbattai Zevi and his followers. It is probably to Luzzatto that he refers there when he says, "And let it be known that we, the children of Israel, do not believe the Kabbalah of the later scholars but only that which was received and verified by the generation that was all knowledge, the days of the saintly Ari of blessed memory." Luzzatto in one of his letters (see Ginzberg, ibid.) claimed to have received mystical lore of the same rank as the Ari.

62. Preface and precept 419, etc.

with their rabbinic interpretation. Ultimately, as is evidenced by his lengthy introduction to the work, his entire approach to Torah is based solely on faith. He continually exhorts to believe. Difficulties, obscurities, contradictions, and failure to understand are all put down to the weakness of the intellect, but faith in Torah in its widest sense must not be weakened because of limited understanding. One senses a certain impatience with the intellectual level for which he wrote, a kind of "they can't understand it anyway" attitude. He concludes one section of his introduction by saying, "If we were able to understand the purpose of the mitzvot, we would rejoice fully. However, when we cannot, we must believe that God who enjoined them knows the purpose of our observing them."

A novel interpretation of the saying "Torah will be forgotten in Israel"[63] is offered in the preface. This to the effect that the statement refers to the subject of TaRYaG, "which has become so obscured that Nachmanides has already declared that Elijah will be required in order to elucidate it clearly." This explanation affords Hagiz the excuse for following, undeviatingly, Maimonides' enumeration.

Hagiz, in spite of his unremitting struggle against mysticism, is a mystic of no mean caliber. Paradoxically enough, even in this work, declared to be for the layman, mysticism plays an important, if not quite decisive, role.

In the preface, mystical themes such as the conception of Torah as representing in reality the names of God in various forms are in evidence, while throughout the work the reasons advanced for the precepts, in the majority of instances, involve mystical reflections. Throughout, one feels that Hagiz the halachist is struggling with Hagiz the

---

63. *Shabbat* 138b.

mystic. He is quite unable to suppress his mystical lore, and it is without doubt these mystical utterances, hints, and flights of fancy that are responsible for stirring the imagination and inspiring religious thought in the work. Beauty and poetry do not form part of his treatment of the precepts; a profound sense of deeper mystery is its essence and is certainly conveyed to the student. Unlike SHeLaH[64] he is often obscure, and on occasion[65] he simply refers one to the *Zohar* itself for further enlightenment.

Afraid of subversive influence, he elaborates at great length in the final precept on the literature to be read by the believing Jew. He roundly condemns certain works[66] as leading to freethinking and warmly recommends others "that lead to the fear of God."[67] The work also contains polemic against J. A. Eisenmenger, who, in 1700, published his infamous attack on Judaism, the *Entdecktes Judenthum*, in which he asserted that rabbinic tradition is anti-Christian and permits stealing from non-Jews.[68]

The work proved popular enough to warrant a second edition during the author's lifetime.

II

Although several works on TaRYaG were written by non-Jews,[69] only one before the Soncino translation of Maimonides' list, published in 1940, appeared in English. It is the

---

64. See earlier in this chapter.

65. For example, precept 531.

66. Such as those of Abraham Cordozo and those of the "well-known serpent his pupil."

67. Such as the Conciliator of Menasseh ben Israel.

68. See precept 564. Cf. also Jellineck K. T., no. 16. Eisenmenger's work was republished in 1711.

69. See Jellineck, K. T., nos. 90, 96, etc.

list reproduced by the apostate from Judaism, Moses Margoliouth, in his "Fundamental Principles of Modern Judaism Investigated."[70]

Margoliouth translated the list contained in "Torath Kattan" (The Law of the Minor[71]), written in 1745 by R. Gedalia of Amsterdam, who published it with object of children "learning it by heart in infancy . . . so that that which they learn in their youthful days they may remember in old age." Margoliouth himself complains[72] of the fact that he had been obliged, when only six or seven years old, to learn this list by heart.

Throughout the work the precepts are discussed in a most disparaging manner. Its sole merit lies, perhaps, in the fact that it is the first TaRYaG list to have appeared in English.

III

A great deal of writing indeed has been done on TaRYaG by mystics. Moses De Leon, alleged author of the *Zohar*, himself wrote a special work on the subject,[73] as did the earlier Kabbalist Ezra Hamekkubal.[74] Isaac Luria, Moses Cordovero, and many others embodied their mystical teaching within a TaRYaG framework,[75] but most important of all is the fact that an entire section of the *Zohar*, the

---

70. London, 1843.

71. Wrongly translated by Margoliouth as "The Law in Miniature."

72. Page 117, note.

73. Or Zarua, manuscript, Oxford, Uri 318. Sefer Harimon, Manus, David Oppenheimer, no. 731.

74. He arranged the mitzvot according to the Decalogue. Menachem Rikanti followed the work of Ezra Hamekkubal closely.

75. Taamei Hamitzvot LeHa'Ari, forming the third part of Nof Etz Chayyim (Salonika, 1852). Taamei Hamitzvot of R. Moses Cordovero, see Shem Hagedolim, pt. 11, no. 94. Metzudath David of Radbaz (Zalkowa, 5622).

Reyah Mehemna (Faithful Shepherd), is devoted to enumerating TaRYaG and offering a mystical treatment and interpretation of the precepts.

This work does not form a continuous element in the *Zohar* but is scattered throughout. According to Jellineck,[76] it was inserted into the *Zohar* at a later date, and an examination of the Reyah would throw much light on the origin of the *Zohar* itself.

The Reyah as we have it is only a fragment of what must have been a much larger work. Reuben Margolies, in his introduction to the *Zohar*,[77] gathers together 158 precepts from the scattered sections and attempts a comparison of this list with those of Maimonides, Nachmanides, and others.

IV

In conclusion, two theories developed by the mystical schools concerning TaRYaG will be mentioned. The one seems to be an extension of the concept underlying the Decalogue–TaRYaG relationship discussed above.[78] The other focuses on the relationship between the individual precept and TaRYaG as a whole in the realm of observance.

Torat HaSefirot (The Law of Divine Grades) plays an important part in medieval Jewish mysticism. It is not possible here to deal with even a single one of the theories concerning them, but our attention is directed toward one aspect of parallelism that is evident in these theories.

---

76. K. T., no. 132.

77. The *Zohar* in three volumes, 2nd ed. (Jerusalem: Mosad HaRav KooK, 1957).

78. Chapter 4.

Cordovero states, "The existence of the Ten Commandments, The Ten Sayings, and the Ten Praises are true witnesses in our Holy Torah for the existence of the Ten Sefirot, without any shadow of doubt."[79] There is in this statement a type of mystical equation between the Decalogue and the Sefirot. In another passage he affirms:[80]

The positive and prohibitive precepts are divided according to, and are dependent upon, the Sefirot.

All of the precepts fit into one of the grades, as we have already seen that they fall under one of the headings of the Decalogue. The Sefirot represent a kind of spiritual ladder both from God to man and from man to God. Combining these ideas, we see that performance of the mitzvot automatically involves one, via the root of the mitzvah in the Decalogue, in the spiritual ascent of the particular Sefirah involved.

The second idea is elaborated upon by Shene Luchoth Habrith, although it is also found in other works and has in fact crept into the prayer book.[81]

It is the idea that in the performance of a single mitzvah one is linked in a spiritual sense with the TaRYaG mitzvot. The theory behind this is again dependent upon the Sefirot. In the same manner that the Sefirot are inextricably mixed with one another, so are the precepts inextricably linked in their spiritual, as opposed to their actual, sense. It is in this sense that all of Israel are able to fulfill the

79. S. Horodetzky, *Torat Hakkabbalah of R. Moses Cordovero* (Berlin, 1884), p. 66.

80. Ibid., p. 302.

81. *Otzar Hatefillot*, p. 882, etc. Cf. the discussion in "Sefer Hai'karrim," third Maamar, chap. 29.

entire Torah, even at the present time. This only applies, however, when one has fulfilled the precept to the maximum of one's ability, and also when the other precepts are incapable of fulfillment, as for example, sacrifices in our day. Shene Luchoth Habrith stresses that maximum performance of the mitzvah includes the study of the mitzvah concerned.

Appendix

As will have become evident from the foregoing chapters, the problems involved in a TaRYaG enumeration are great indeed. While the scope of the present work prevents an exhaustive, detailed treatment of the manner in which various authorities compiled their TaRYaG lists, I feel that the work would be incomplete without the comparative tables that follow.

These tables have been so drawn up that they enable the student to see at a glance which of Maimonides' list of TaRYaG—represented by number only—are included or excluded by different authorities. For purposes of this comparison, and also to evidence as far as possible the effect of Maimonides' work, three pre-Maimonidean and three post-Maimonidean authors have been presented in the tables.

It should be borne in mind that even when particular precepts are included by the various lists, in many instances there are different interpretations of the precise meaning of the precept as well as in its application. Essential notes have also been appended to the tables with the object of clarifying the lists as far as possible.

While every care has been taken in this laborious task, error may well have crept into tables, which involve hundreds of details. I would therefore suggest that whereever possible the student endeavor to check them for himself. Additional matters relevant to the tables are to be found in the body of the work and the notes thereon.

COMPARATIVE TABLES SHOWING WHICH PRECEPTS INCLUDED IN MAIMONIDES' LIST ARE OMITTED BY OTHER AUTHORITIES

Positive Commandments

Halachot Gedolot	Saadya Gaon	Elijah Hazaken	Maimonides	Nachmanides	Sefer Mitzvot HaGadol	Zohar Harakiah	Notes
—	—		1			—	
—	—	—	2			—	
	—		3				
			4			—	
			5	—			
	—		6				
	—		7	—		—	Ra'aBaD also omits this precept.
	—		8				
	—		9				
—			10				Nachmanides considers there to be two precepts here.
			11				Elijah Hazaken has eight precepts here.

Halachot Gedolot	Saadya Gaon	Elijah Hazaken	Maimonides	Nachmanides	Sefer Mitzvot HaGadol	Zohar Harakiah	Notes
			12				*Halachot Gedolot* includes no. 13, as does Elijah Hazaken.
—			13				
			14			—	Zohar Harakiah has an additional precept here.
			15				
			16				
		—	17				
			18				
—			19				
			20				Nachmanides and Zohar Harakiah have an additional precept here.
—		—	21				
—	—		22				
			23				
—			24				
			25				Halachot Gedolot includes no. 33 here.
			26				

					Notes
27					
28					Halachot Gedolot includes no. 35 here. Nachmanides considers this to be two precepts.
29	—			—	
30	—			—	
31	—		—		
32	—			—	Zohar Harakiah has an additional precept here.
33	—			—	
34	—	—		—	
35	—			—	
36	—			—	
37	—			—	
38				—	
39		—			Nachmanides considers this to be two precepts.
40					

Continued

173

Halachot Gedolot	Saadya Gaon	Elijah Hazaken	Maimonides	Nachmanides	Sefer Mitzvot HaGadol	Zohar Harakiah	Notes
	—		41				Elijah Hazaken includes all the *Musaphim* as a single precept thus including 42, 43, 45, 47, 50, and 51. Halachot Gedolot includes nos. 41, 42, 43, 45, 47, 48, 50, and 51.
—	—	—	42				
—	—	—	43				
—			44				
—	—	—	45				
		—	46				
—	—	—	47				
—	—	—	48				
			49				
—	—	—	50				Elijah Hazaken includes *Nissuch Hamayim* here.
—	—	—	51				
		—	52				
			53				
			54				

				Remarks
55	—	—		Elijah Hazaken has two precepts here.
56				
57	—	—		
58	—			
59	—	—		See Ra'aBaD's remarks.
60				
61				
62			—	
63	—			Elijah Hazaken includes no. 66. Halachot Gedolot includes nos. 66 and 67. Elijah Hazaken includes no. 72.
64	—		—	
65	—	—	—	
66	—		—	
67	—			
68				
69	—			Halachot Gedolot includes nos. 70, 71, and 72.

Continued

175

Halachot Gedolot	Saadya Gaon	Elijah Hazaken	Maimonides	Nachmanides	Sefer Mitzvot HaGadol	Zohar Harakiah	Notes
—		—	70				Elijah Hazaken includes no. 70 here.
—	—		71				
—	—	—	72				
		—	73				
—		—	74				
—		—	75				
—		—	76				
—	—	—	77				
			78				
			79				
			80				
			81				
—	—		82			—	
			83				
—	—	—	84				
—	—	—	85	—		—	
—	—	—	86				
—	—	—	87				
—	—	—	88				

			No.			Notes
—		—	89			
—	—	—	90			
			91			
—		—	92			
—		—	93			Halachot Gedolot includes no. 93.
			94			Nachmanides considers this to be two precepts.
		—	95	—	—	Halachot Gedolot includes 98 and 97.
—		—	96	—	—	Elijah Hazaken includes 97.
—			97	—	—	
			98	—	—	
			99	—	—	Elijah Hazaken and Sefer Mitzvot HaKatzar have an additional precept here.
—			100	—	—	Elijah Hazaken includes 77 here.
—			101	—	—	Halachot Gedolot includes 102 and 103.
			102	—	—	
			103	—	—	

Continued

Halachot Gedolot	Saadya Gaon	Elijah Hazaken	Maimonides	Nachmanides	Sefer Mitzvot HaGadol	Zohar Harakiah	Notes
			104	—		—	Elijah Hazaken includes 74, 75, and 106. Halachot Gedolot includes 106, 99, and 105.
—		—	105	—		—	
—		—	106	—		—	
	—	—	107	—		—	Zohar Harakiah has *taharat hamet* in place of no. 107.
		—	108	—		—	Ra'aBaD considers this to be two precepts.
			109				
			110				Elijah Hazaken includes 76, 111, and 112.
—		—	111				
—	—	—	112				
			113			—	Elijah Hazaken includes 107 and 108.
		—	114				Halachot Gedolot includes nos. 115, 116, and 117.
—		—	115				
—		—	116				

Continued

117				—	
118					
119			—		—
120		—			
121		—			
122		—			
123		—			
124					
125	—	—			
126					
127					
128					

Elijah Hazaken and Halachot Gedolot consider the five fifths as five separate precepts.

Elijah Hazaken considers 120 and 121 to contain two precepts each: one for *field*; one for *trees*.

Elijah Hazaken considers also *shikchah bekerem* and *peah bekerem*.

Nachmanides has two precepts here. Nachmanides has two precepts here. Elijah Hazaken, Halachot Gedolot, and Zohar Harakiah have two precepts here.

179

Halachot Gedolot	Saadya Gaon	Elijah Hazaken	Maimonides	Nachmanides	Sefer Mitzvot HaGadol	Zohar Harakiah	Notes
		—	129				
			130				Nachmanides has two precepts here.
			131				
			132				
			133				Nachmanides considers there to be two precepts here.
	—	—	134				Zohar Harakiah and Nachmanides have an additional precept here.
			135				Elijah Hazaken includes in nos. 135, 136, and 139 the precepts in nos. 134, 137, 138, and 140. He also has an additional precept here.
	—	—	136				
		—	137				
—			138				
	—		139				
	—		140				
			141				

		No.				Remarks
—	—	142		—	—	See Mitzvot Hashem 478 and note thereon.
		143				
		144				
		145				
—		146		—	—	See also Ra'aBaD's remarks. Elijah Hazaken and Halachot Gedolot add *shechitat kodeshim*. Halachot Gedolot omits *shechitat chullin*.
		147				
	—	148				
—	—	149	—	—	—	Ra'aBaD also omits nos. 149, 150, 151, and 152.
—	—	150	—	—	—	
—	—	151	—	—	—	
—	—	152	—	—	—	
		153				Nachmanides considers this to be two precepts, as does Sefer Mitzvot HaGadol positive commandments 46–47.
	—	154				

Continued

Halachot Gedolot	Saadya Gaon	Elijah Hazaken	Maimonides	Nachmanides	Sefer Mitzvot HaGadol	Zohar Harakiah	Notes
			155				
			156				
—		—	157				Zohar Harakiah has an additional precept here.
			158				Elijah Hazaken has eating *marror* as a separate precept.
			159				
			160				
			161				
			162				
			163	—			
			164	—			
			165				Nachmanides considers this to be two prohibitions.
			166				
			167				
			168				
			169				
			170				
—	—		171				
			172				

182

			No.	Notes
			173	
			174	
—	—	—	175	
			176	— Halachot Gedolot includes 232, 233, and 234.
			177	Possibly meant by Elijah Hazaken when he says "bringing peace between the parties"
—	—	—	178	Sefer Mitzvot HaKatzar 238 lists this as a prohibition.
			179	
—	—	—	180	
			181	Ra'aBaD omits this precept.
			182	
			183	
			184	
			185	Sefer Mitzvot Hakatzar 37 deduces *seven* precepts from the verse. Elijah Hazaken has *two* precepts.
—	—	—	186	
			187	
			188	

Continued

Halachot Gedolot	Saadya Gaon	Elijah Hazaken	Maimonides	Nachmanides	Sefer Mitzvot HaGadol	Zohar Harakiah	Notes
—		—	189				Elijah Hazaken includes 190.
		—	190				
—	—	—	191				Halachot Gedolot, Elijah Hazaken, and Sefer Mitzvot HaGadol include 193 in this precept.
			192				
—	—	—	193	—			Elijah Hazaken, *Halachot Gedolot*, Nachmanides, and *Zohar Harakiah* consider there to be two precepts here.
	—		194				
	—		195				
			196				
			197				
—		—	198	—	—		Ra'aBaD also omits this precept. Elijah Hazaken and Halachot Gedolot consider also *the acceptance of a pledge* to be a precept.
			199				

					Notes
200				—	
201			—	—	
202			—		
203					
204					
205					
206					
207			—		Elijah Hazaken has three precepts here.
208					Elijah Hazaken has two precepts here.
209					Sefer Mitzvot Hakatzar considers this as two precepts 51–52. Elijah Hazaken adds *fearing the wise.* Halachot Gedolot has two precepts.
210		—			
211		—			
212		—			
213			—	—	
214	—		—	—	Sefer Mitzvot Hakatzar considers this precept to refer to *conjugal rights.*

Continued

Halachot Gedolot	Saadya Gaon	Elijah Hazaken	Maimonides	Nachmanides	Sefer Mitzvot HaGadol	Zohar Harakiah	Notes
		—	215				Zohar Harakiah has an additional precept here.
		—	216				
—	—		217				Elijah Hazaken includes no. 220.
	—		218				
	—		219				
	—	—	220				According to Saadya, this is listed with the prohibitions. So also 224 and 239.
			221				
			222				
			223			—	
—	—		224				
—	—	—	225	—			Nachmanides and Zohar Harakiah consider four types of capital punishment as a single precept.
—	—	—	226			—	

186

						No.		Notes
—			—			227	—	Elijah Hazaken and Halachot Gedolot consider each case in 226, 227, 228, and 229 as a separate precept, making a total of 71 punishments.
—	—		—			228	—	
—	—	—				229	—	
—						230		
—						231		
—					—	232		Elijah Hazaken has two precepts here: one when the court sells; the other when he sells himself. Elijah Hazaken includes no. 234.
—						233		
—			—			234		
—			—			235		
—						236	—	Elijah Hazaken includes 237, 239 (pt.) 238, 240, 241, 242, 243, and 244. Halachot Gedolot includes 237, 238, 239, 240, 241, 242, 243, 244, 245, and 246.

Continued

187

Halachot Gedolot	Saadya Gaon	Elijah Hazaken	Maimonides	Nachmanides	Sefer Mitzvot HaGadol	Zohar Harakiah	Notes
—		—		237		—	Zohar Harakiah replaces these ten precepts with one: *to judge righteously.*
—		—	238			—	Ra'aBaD omits this precept.
—	—	—	239			—	
—		—	240			—	
—		—	241			—	
—		—	242			—	
—		—	243			—	
—		—	244			—	
—	—	—	245			—	
—	—	—	246			—	
—		—	247			—	Nachmanides and Zohar Harakiah consider a second precept and a prohibition in connection with this precept.
—			248				

COMPARATIVE TABLES SHOWING WHICH PRECEPTS INCLUDED IN MAIMONIDES' LIST ARE OMITTED BY OTHER AUTHORITIES

Prohibitions

Halachot Gedolot	Saadya Gaon	Elijah Hazaken	Maimonides	Nachmanides	Sefer Mitzvot HaGadol	Zohar Harakiah	Notes
		—	1				Nachmanides considers 1, 2, 5, and 6 to be a single prohibition.
	—		2	—			
		—	3				Zohar Harakiah explains prohibition against retaining them in existence.
—	—		4				
		—	5	—			
—		—	6	—		—	
			7			—	
			8				Zohar Harakiah includes no. 9 in this.
			9			—	

189

Halachot Gedolot	Saadya Gaon	Elijah Hazaken	Maimonides	Nachmanides	Sefer Mitzvot HaGadol	Zohar Harakiah	Notes
—	—	—	10				
			11				
			12				
			13				
			14		—		Sefer Mitzvot Hafadol includes this in prohibition 26. See Sefer Mitzvot HaGadol 32.
—	—		15				
—	—		16				
—	—		17				
—	—		18				
—	—	—	19				
			20				
			21				
			22				
—			23				
			24				
			25				
	—		26				
	—		27				
			28	—		—	

190

29	—		—
30			
31	—		
32			
33			
34	—		
35	—		
36			—
37			—
38			—
39			—
40			
41			
42			
43	Ra'aBaD has four prohibitions here.		
44			
45			
46		—	
47	Elijah Hazaken has two prohibitions here.	—	
48			

Continued

Halachot Gedolot	Saadya Gaon	Elijah Hazaken	Maimonides	Nachmanides	Sefer Mitzvot HaGadol	Zohar Harakiah	Notes
	—		49				
	—		50				
	—	—	51				Sefer Mitzvot HaGadol holds that this refers only to the seven nations. See 49.
			52				Elijah Hazaken has two prohibitions here.
			53				Nachmanides considers this to embrace two prohibitions, as does Sefer Mitzvot HaGadol, 113–114, and Elijah Hazaken.
	—		54				
	—		55				
			56				
			57				Elijah Hazaken and Halachot Gedolot have two prohibitions here.
	—		58	—			Ra'aBaD considers this a divine promise and not a warning.
—			59				
—			60				
	—		61				

192

					Notes
62					
63	—				
64	—				
65	—				
66	—				
67	—	—	—	—	Sefer Mitzvot HaGadol includes this in Maimonides' positive commandment 22. See Sefer Mitzvot HaGadol, positive commandment 165.
68	—	—			Zohar Harakiah has a further prohibition here.
69	—				
70	—	—	—	—	Nachmanides and Sefer Mitzvot HaGadol consider 70 and 71 to be a single prohibition. Sefer Mitzvot HaGadol 308.
71	—	—	—	—	

Continued

Halachot Gedolot	Saadya Gaon	Elijah Hazaken	Maimonides	Nachmanides	Sefer Mitzvot HaGadol	Zohar Harakiah	Notes
—	—	—	72				Zohar Harakia has an additional prohibition here.
			73				
		—	74				
	—		75				
			76				
	—		77				
			78		—		Sefer Mitzvot HaGadol includes this with Maimonides' positive commandment 31.
	—		79				
			80				
		—	81				
—			82				
—			83				
			84				
			85				
	—		86				
	—		87				
—		—	88				
	—		89				

194

Continued

					Notes
90					
91					Nachmanides includes 91, 92, 93, and 94 here.
92	—				
93	—				
94	—				
95	—				Sefer Mitzvot HaGadol includes this with his prohibition 313.
96	—				Elijah Hazaken includes no. 97 here.
97					
98					Nachmanides as Sefer Mitzvot HaGadol (318–319), Elijah Hazaken, and Zohar Harakiah consider this to be two prohibitions.
99					
100					Nachmanides and Sefer Mitzvot HaGadol (316–317) consider this to be two prohibitions.

195

Halachot Gedolot	Saadya Gaon	Elijah Hazaken	Maimonides	Nachmanides	Sefer Mitzvot HaGadol	Zohar Harakiah	Notes
			101				
—		—	102			—	
—		—	103			—	
—	—	—	104				Zohar Harakiah includes in 104 and 105 the prohibitions in 102 and 103.
	—	—	105				
—		—	106				
—			107				
	—	—	108				
—	—	—	109				
—	—	—	110				
		—	111				
—			112				
—			113				
			114				
			115				
			116				
		—	117				Halachot Gedolot has two prohibitions here.
	—	—	118				
—	—	—	119				

196

120	121	122	123	124	125	126	127	128	129	130	131	132	133	134	135	136	137	138	139
I	I	I		I					I			I	I		I		I		I
		I		I							I		I	I					
		I		I									I	I			I		

197

Halachot Gedolot	Saadya Gaon	Elijah Hazaken	Maimonides	Nachmanides	Sefer Mitzvot HaGadol	Zohar Harakiah	Notes
	—	—	140		—		See Sefer Mitzvot HaGadol, prohibition 264. Nachmanides considers nos. 141, 142, and 143 to be a single precept.
		—	141				
—	—	—	142	—		—	
—	—	—	143	—		—	
—	—	—	144			—	
—	—	—	145			—	
—	—	—	146			—	
—	—	—	147			—	
—			148			—	Chinuch omits this prohibition, including it in Chinuch 280.
—	—	—	149	—		—	
			150	—	—	—	Sefer Mitzvot HaGadol considers this a prohibition affecting all sacred food (not as Maimonides).
			151				
			152				
	—		153	—		—	
			154			—	

Nachmanides and Sefer Mitzvot HaGadol (350–351) consider this to be two prohibitions.

155

156
157
158
159
160
161
162
163
164
165
166

Elijah Hazaken and Sefer Mitzvot HaGadol (234–235) consider this to be two prohibitions.

167
168

Continued

199

Halachot Gedolot	Saadya Gaon	Elijah Hazaken	Maimonides	Nachmanides	Sefer Mitzvot HaGadol	Zohar Harakiah	Notes
—			169				
—	—		170				
			171				
			172				
		—	173				
		—	174				
			175				
		—	176				
—	—	—	177	—	—	—	
—	—	—	178	—	—	—	
			179	—		—	Nachmanides includes this in 173.
			180				
			181			—	
			182				
			183				
			184				Zohar Harakiah has two prohibitions here.
			185				
			186				

200

187	—	—	—			Elijah Hazaken and Zohar Harakiah have a further prohibition here.
188	—	—				
189	—					Nachmanides considers 190 and 191 included here. Sefer Mitzvot HaGadol 119. Halachot Gedolot includes 190 and 191. Zohar Harakiah includes 190 and 191.
190	—	—	—		—	
191	—	—	—		—	
192				—		Sefer Mitzvot HaGadol considers 192 and 193 to be a single prohibition.
193	—	—				
194	—	—				
195	—	—	—		—	Nachmanides and Zohar Harakiah have two prohibitions here.
196	—	—				

Continued

Halachot Gedolot	Saadya Gaon	Elijah Hazaken	Maimonides	Nachmanides	Sefer Mitzvot HaGadol	Zohar Harakiah	Notes
			197				
—	—		198	—		—	
—	—		199	—	—	—	Sefer Mitzvot HaGadol (prohibition 76) is doubtful.
			200				Sefer Mitzvot HaGadol and Elijah Hazaken have two prohibitions here.
			201				
			202				Elijah Hazaken has an additional prohibition "*chometz yayin*"
			203				Sefer Mitzvot HaGadol and Zohar Harakiah include 204.
		—	204			—	
		—	205				
—		—	206				Sefer Mitzvot HaGadol and Zohar Harakiah include 206.
	—		207				
	—	—	208			—	
	—		209				
			210				
			211				

212					
213					
214	Halachot Gedolot and Elijah Hazaken have two prohibitions here.			—	
215					
216					
217					
218				—	
219					
220					
221					
222					
223					
224	Sefer Mitzvot				
225					
226				—	
227				—	—
228		—		—	—
229					—
230					

Continued

Halachot Gedolot	Saadya Gaon	Elijah Hazaken	Maimonides	Nachmanides	Sefer Mitzvot HaGadol	Zohar Harakiah	Notes
		—	231				Elijah Hazaken has two prohibitions here.
			232				
	—		233				
			234				
			235				Elijah Hazaken has two prohibitions here.
			236				
			237				
			238				
	—		239				
		—	240				
			241				
	—		242				Sefer Mitzvot HaGadol (189–190) considers this to be two prohibitions.
			243				
—			244				
			245				

204

Continued

246				Sefer Mitzvot HaGadol (156) is doubtful concerning this prohibition.
247	—			
248			—	
249	—	—		
250			—	
251				
252				
253				
254				Sefer Mitzvot HaGadol (180) is doubtful about 254 and 255 being separate.
255	—	—		Nachmanides considers this to be two prohibitions, as does Sefer Mitzvot Hakatzar (86–87). Sefer Mitzvot HaGadol (8) is doubtful. Elijah Hazaken has two prohibitions.
256				
257	—	—		

Halachot Gedolot	Saadya Gaon	Elijah Hazaken	Maimonides	Nachmanides	Sefer Mitzvot HaGadol	Zohar Harakiah	Notes
	—	—	258				
			259				
—	—	—	260				
			261				Sefer Mitzvot Hakatzar (276–277) considers this to be two prohibitions.
	—		262				
	—		263				
			264				
	—		265				
	—		266		—		Sefer Mitzvot HaGadol (prohibition 266) includes this with no. 265.
			267				
		—	268				
			269			—	Halachot Gedolot has two prohibitions here.
			270				Elijah Hazaken has two prohibitions here, as do Halachot Gedolot and Zohar Harakiah.
			271				
			272				

						Notes
273						
274						
275						
276						
277						
278	—		—			
279	—	—			—	
280		—				
281						
282						
283			—			Ra'aBaD disagrees. Elijah Hazakiah understands this prohibition differently, as does Sefer Mitzvot HaGadol 196.
284						
285	—					
286						
287		—		—		

Continued

Halachot Gedolot	Saadya Gaon	Elijah Hazaken	Maimonides	Nachmanides	Sefer Mitzvot HaGadol	Zohar Harakiah	Notes
	—		288				Sefer Mitzvot HaGadol considers this prohibition to refer to the witnesses, and not, as Maimonides, to the court.
			289				Halachot Gedolot has two prohibitions here.
			290				Nachmanides considers this to contain two prohibitions.
—	—		291		—		See Sefer Mitzvot HaGadol, prohibition 264. Nachmanides has an additional prohibition here.
	—	—	292				
—	—		293			—	Nachmanides and Zohar Harakiah have an additional prohibition here.
—	—	—	294		—	—	
—		—	295				
—		—	296				
			297				
	—		298				
			299				
	—		300				

208

					Notes
301	—	—	—		
302					
303					
304					
305					
306					
307	—	—	—	—	Nachmanides includes this under Maimonides' prohibition 308, as does Zohar Harakiah.
308			—		
309					
310		—	—		
311					Nachmanides, Elijah Hazakiah, and Halachot Gedolot consider this to be two prohibitions.
312		—			
313		—	—		

Continued

Halachot Gedolot	Saadya Gaon	Elijah Hazaken	Maimonides	Nachmanides	Sefer Mitzvot HaGadol	Zohar Harakiah	Notes
—			314				
			315				
			316				
			317				Sefer Mitzvot HaGadol, Elijah Hazaken, and Yeraim add "not to curse oneself."
	—	—	318				
	—		319	—			Nachmanides considers this included in prohibition 300.
			320				
		—	321	—		—	
		—	322				
			323				
			324				
			325				
			326				
			327				
			328				
			329				
			330				
			331				

	332	
	333	
	334	
	335	
	336	
	337	Halachot Gedolot includes two further prohibitions here.
	338	
	339	
	340	Sefer Mitzvot HaGadol considers there to be two prohibitions here (118–119).
	341	
	342	
	343	
	344	
	345	
	346	
	347	Halachot Gedolot has a further prohibition here.
	348	
	349	

Continued

Halachot Gedolot	Saadya Gaon	Elijah Hazaken	Maimonides	Nachmanides	Sefer Mitzvot HaGadol	Zohar Harakiah	Notes
			350				
—	—		351				
—	—	—	352	—			
—	—	—	353				
			354			—	Possibly Elijah Hazaken has two prohibitions here.
			355				Elijah Hazaken considers there to be two prohibitions here. See note in Mitzvot Hashem, 570.
			356				Nachmanides considers there to be two prohibitions here.
			357				
			358				
			359				
			360				
			361				
	—		362				
			363				
			364				
			365				

212

Bibliography

AARON HALEVI
OF BARCELONA

—Sefer Hachinuch.
—1st. ed Venice 1523,
critically edited by C. D.
Chavel. 4th ed. Jer. 1960.
—Bomberg 1523.
—Frankfurt On Oder 1783.
—Various ed. with
commentaries Minchath
Chinuch. MaHaRaM Shick,
etc.

AZHAROT

ANONYMOUS

—Atta Hinchalta—Ashkenazi
Machzor.

ANONYMOUS

—Azharat Reshit—Ashkenazi
Machzor.

ANONYMOUS   —Maamar Haskel—ed.
                         Cremona 1577. ed.
                         Rodelheim 1804.
ALGERBELONI, I.   —Ayzeh Mekom Binah, ed.
                         with short notes by Isaac b.
                         Amrug, in Minchath
                         Bikkurim, Livorno 1837.
                         —Machzor Algier, Livorno
                         1650.
ELIJAH HAZAKEN   —Emet Yehege Chikki.
                         —ed. with introduction and
                         notes by M. Slutzky,
                         Warsaw 1900.
IBN GABIROL   —Shemor Libbi Maaneh.
                         —According to Livorno 1837.
                         —According to Zohar
                         Harakia, Vilna 1879.
                         —According to various
                         Machzorim
SAADYA GAON   —Esh Ochela in Kovetz
                         Maaseh Yede Geonim.
                         Berlin 1856.

LATER AZHAROT
BENVENISTE, JOSHUA   —En Passante
CHAIM B. ZEBULUN   —Shira Lemoshe. Warsaw
                         1814.
EYBESCHUTZ, J.   —Shirat Mitzvot, Prague
                         1765.
KIMCHI, ISAAC   —En Passante
MEISEL, M.   —Shirat Moshe. Shklov 1788.

AZKARI, E.   —Charedim Lemberg 1859.
                              —1st ed. Venice 1599.
ABRIDGED VERSION   —A Danzig. Vilna 1817.
CHAVEL, C. B.   —The Book of Divine
                              Precepts, Soncino 1940.
CORDOVERO, M.   —Taamei Hamitzvot.
DANIEL HABABLI   —Maasseh Nissim. Paris
                              1867.
DURAN, S.   —Zohar Harakia, Vilna 1879.
ELIEZER OF METZ   —Yeraim. ed. by Benjamin
                              The Physician, Venice
                              1565.
YERAIM HASHALEM   —Ed. A. A. Schiff,
                              1894–1904.
GEDALIA OF   —Torath Kattan. Amsterdam
AMSTERDAM   1745.
HAGIZ, M.   —Eyleh *HaMitzvot*.
                              Premislan 1903.
HALACHOT GEDOLOT   —Ed. A. S. Traub. Warsaw
                              1874.
                              —Ed. Hildersheimer 1890.
HALPERIN, B.   —Mitzvot HaShem, Frankfurt
                              1857.
HEFETZ b. YATZLIACH   —Book of Precepts.
                              Manuscript edited by
                              Halper in the *Jewish
                              Quarterly Review* 1915.
HOROWITZ, I.   —Shene Luchot Habrit,
                              Frankfurt 1857.

KAGAN, I. M.   —*Sefer HaMitzvot* Hakatzer.
(Chafetz Chayyim)   Jer. 1960.

KALENBERG, J. J.   —*Seder HaMitzvot*, 1861.

LURIA, I.   —Taamei Hamitzvot.
                           Zalkowa 1775. Salonika
                           1852.

MAIMONIDES   —*Sefer HaMitzvot*, ed. C.
                           Heller N.Y. 1946.
                           —With commentary Yad
                           Halevi, I.S. Hurwitz, Jer.
                           1931.
                           —With commentary
                           Machshevet Moshe, Vilna
                           1865.
                           —Ed. Lemberg, 1860, with
                           usual commentaries.
                           —Arabic ed. M. Bloch, Paris
                           1888.
                           —Latin ed. 13th Century.
                           —French ed. M. Bloch, Paris
                           1888.
                           —Italian ed. Venice 1648.
                           —German ed. Prague 1798—
                           I.H. Landau.

MOINESTER J.L.   —*Seder HaMitzvot*, N.Y.
                           1945.

MOSES OF CORBEIL   —SeMaK. Kopys 1820.
                           —Critical ed. I.I. Shapiro. Jer.
                           1959.
                           —Abridged ed. Cracow 1579.

MOSES OF COUCY   —SeMaG. Venice 1522.
                           —Numerous editions.

MOSES DE LEON

—Or Zarua. Manuscript Oxford Uri. 318.
—Sefer Harimon. Manuscript D. Oppenheimer No. 731.

NACHMANIDES

—Sefer Hamitzvot— According to usual editions of Maimonides' S.H.
—TaRYaG Precepts in works. Ed. Chavell Jer. 1964.

REYA MEHEMNA

—In, The Zohar, ed. Margolies. Jer. 1957.

SAADYA GAON

—Ed. Y.P. Perle, Warsaw, 1906–9.
—Sefer Hamitzvot. Ed. S. Halpern. Jer. 1930.

SABBATAI HACOHEN

—Poel Tzedek, Jessnitz 1720.
—In Pe'er Hamitzvot N.Y. 1948.

SHEILTOT

—Jer. 1955.

Shemuel B. Chofni

—Only fragments are preserved of his *Sefer HaMitzvot.*

VITTAL, D.

—Ketter Torah. Jer. 1882.

Index

ABOUT THE AUTHOR

Rabbi Abraham Hirsch Rabinowitz was a well-known author and scholar. An alumnus of Gateshead Yeshiva and Hebron Yeshiva, he received rabbinical ordination from Chief Rabbi Hertzog, Rabbi Meltzer, and Rabbi Sarna. He attained academic degrees from Leeds University and the University of Witwatersrand. He served as rabbi to distinguished communities in England and South Africa. In 1961, he returned to Israel with his family, and in 1968 he was appointed chief rabbi of the Israeli air force. Rabbi Rabinowitz contributed widely to periodicals and encyclopedias on various Jewish and general topics. His books include *The Jewish Mind, Israel: The Christian Dilemma, Science Today—Religion Tomorrow* (unpublished), *Hamitzvah Vehamikra, The Study of Talmud: Understanding the Halachic Mind,* and the award-winning *Olam Ehad.* He prepared and edited the momentous *Ali Tamar*, a seven-volume commentary on the Jerusalem Talmud, written by his father-in-law, Rabbi Yisachar Tamar. Rabbi Rabinowitz died in 1987.